The Information Economy
and American Cities

The Information Economy
and American Cities

Matthew P. Drennan

THE JOHNS HOPKINS UNIVERSITY PRESS
BALTIMORE AND LONDON

To my wife, Katherine Van Wezel Stone
and to Erica, Grace, and Ava

The Johns Hopkins University Press
2715 North Charles Street
Baltimore, Maryland 21218-4363
www.press.jhu.edu

Library of Congress Cataloging-in-Publication Data

Drennan, Matthew P., 1937–
    The information economy and American cities /
Matthew P. Drennan.
        p.   cm.
    Includes bibliographical references and index.
    ISBN 0-8018-6934-X
    1. Information technology—Economic aspects—United
States.   2. Metropolitan areas—United States.
3. United States—Economic conditions—1981–2001.
4. United States—Economic conditions—1971–1981
5. United States—Economic conditions—1961–1971.
6. Urban economics.   I. Title.
    HC110.I55 D73 2002
    307.76′0973—dc21   2001004976

A catalog record for this book is available from the British
Library.

Contents

| Tables and Figures

Tables

Figures

| Preface and Acknowledgments

The information sector is the most dynamic part of the U.S. economy. The firms and nonprofit organizations included in the information sector represent over 30% of the nation's gross domestic product, about the same size as the goods production sector. In 1950, the information sector represented 12% of the national economy, while the goods production sector represented 54%. This book documents the rise of the information sector in the U.S. economy and explores the implications of that rise for the economies of metropolitan areas.

In the information sector, unlike in traditional sectors—agriculture, mining, manufacturing, and distribution—information is both a major input and an output. The final products of the information sector are services, not goods, and those services are information intensive. Some services, such as haircutting and auto repair, are not intensive users of information; so the information sector described here is not the same as what has been called the service economy, an amorphous catch-all that includes everything from financial hedge funds to candy stores.

Many large metropolitan areas that formerly specialized in the production and distribution of goods that were exported to regional, national, and even international markets now specialize in the information sector. Just as goods can be exported, information products can be exported and thus generate the income required to support the local economic activities of a metropolitan area, such as retail trade, construction, and government. The output of information sector firms such as banks, law firms, and computer software producers is not loaded onto trucks, airplanes, and trains for shipment beyond the metropolitan area, but much of it is sold to nonlocal customers. The traditional conception in planning and regional economics that manufacturing is the "basic" or "export" activity of an urban economy while all services are "nonbasic" or "local" presumes that the only source of export income for urban economies is the sale of goods to the rest of the world. If that were the case, huge, prosperous metropoplitan areas such as San Francisco and Boston would collapse, because their "basic" sector of manufacturing has shriveled to a tiny share of their urban economies. In fact their thriving export activities are the production of information sector services.

The decline of manufacturing as an important export sector in many metropolitan areas, such as San Francisco and Boston, does not mean that U.S. manufacturing output is in decline. It is not. But manufacturing has not been growing as fast as the information sector, and it has become more dispersed, spreading to smaller metropolitan areas and outside of metropolitan areas altogether. Some have argued that the replacement in large cities of manufacturing by the information sector, a "yuppie" economy, has been a disaster for poor minorities. My data reveal that the opposite is the case. The transformation of metropolitan economies, especially the large ones, from specialization in the export of goods to specialization in the export of information services, is manifest in many visible ways. The formerly working waterfronts of many port cities, rendered obsolete by changes in distribution technology, have been made over as upper-middle-class attractions and neighborhoods, providing upscale shopping, dining, and sports with a water view. In the 1950s, longshoremen in steel-toed shoes, carrying their hooks, streamed down West 14th Street in Manhattan every morning on their way to the Hudson River piers. Today, investment bankers with their Palm Pilots and Nike running shoes head to the same piers even earlier in the morning for tennis, running, workouts, or power breakfasts. Similarly, the Chicago evoked by Carl Sandburg, "City of the Big Shoulders," has vanished. In its place is a city of sharp elbows in tailored suits.

Does the crash of high-technology stocks in 2000–2001 herald the imminent decline of the information sector as the major force driving metropolitan economies? The information sector described here is not the creature of Wall Street hype. It is not the "new economy" or the "high-tech sector" touted by the media and embraced, and then shunned, by investors. It does not include high-tech manufacturers of computers, such as Dell, Compaq, and IBM, or the manufacturers of telecommunication equipment, such as Lucent, Corning, and Nortel. Nor does it include the dot-com retailers, such as Amazon.com and the now-defunct Webvan.com and Pet.com. Yet there is some overlap—although it is relatively small—between the information sector as defined here and what has been variously called the "information economy" the "new economy" and the "high-tech sector." For example, the information sector includes software producers, such as Microsoft and Netscape, and telecommunication providers, such as AT&T, Verizon, and Sprint, many of which suffered huge losses in share value during the 2000–2001 stampede out of the sector that the financial markets loosely call high-tech stocks.

High-tech stocks are heavily concentrated on the NASDAQ stock exchange. The meltdown of the NASDAQ that began in March 2000 has wiped out two trillion dollars in stock market value and rendered millions of stock options worthless, even before destruction of the World Trade Center pushed stocks down. Many of the dot-com firms of the late 1990s are now history: 220 shut down in 2000 and 332 shut down in the first half of 2001. One-third of the dot-coms that have shut down were located in the Silicon Valley area, the heart of the high-tech economy.

Despite the huge losses in share value among high-tech firms, the information sector as defined here is *not* in decline. The parts of the information sector that were hit by the drop in high-tech stocks represent a small piece of the total. The other parts of the information sector, both firms and nonprofit organizations, are not included in the new economy before the stock market crash. Those other parts include banks, insurance companies, financial service firms, universities, medical centers, motion picture production, law firms, accounting firms, management consultancies, and museums, among others. What those diverse activities have in common is that information is both a major input and a major output, they employ a highly educated work force, and they have been expanding faster than the goods production sector for at least one-half century. Collectively, at the end of the twentieth century, the information sector is as large as the goods production sector in the United States. Although the information sector produces services, it is not the same as the service economy broadly defined. It does not include routine services like hotels, repair services, personal services, and social services. Nor does it include any of retail trade or government or construction or electric and gas utilities.

The information sector flourishes in our largest urban areas, especially the downtowns of big cities. In the aftermath of the destruction of the World Trade Center by terrorists, some observers are deeply discounting downtown locations; but massive dispersion of information sector firms to small places is simply not a viable option, as it clearly has been and remains for manufacturing firms. The economic gains achieved by informatin sector firms from clustering together in large cities are simply too great to be sacrificed in an emotional search for safety.

In writing this book, I have benefited from the helpful and incisive comments of Dick Netzer on an earlier draft. Similarly, Tom Stanback and R. D. (Pat) Norton read an earlier version, and both contributed improvements. José Lobo, my colleague and collaborator at Cornell University, has contributed to this effort through many discussions of the themes in this book. I am grateful to Professors Walter Isard and Sid Saltzman of Cornell for providing me a number of opportunities to present parts of this research in their Regional Science seminar. Saurav Dev Bhatta, a former doctoral student and now a professor at the University of Illinois, I thank for performing the input-output analysis I used. I thank Doug Rae of the Yale School of Management for setting me up as a visiting fellow, providing me with the perfect sabbatical for getting work done. Also, Erica Groshen, Joe Tracy, and James Orr, all of the New York Federal Reserve Bank, provided me with a New York office, computer, and fabulous library the one day per week I was not at Yale. Porus Olpadwala, my dean at the College of Architecture, Art, and Planning at Cornell University, provided generous support, both moral and financial, for this research. Thomas Otto, a graduate student, produced far nicer figures than I possibly could, in addition to providing last-minute research assistance. I wish that I could write as carefully, and as swiftly, as Helena Wood can process words. She typed the mnauscript far more than once. Finally, I thank my wife, Katherine Van Wezel Stone, for urging me some years ago to write this book and for facilitating my efforts.

The Information Economy
and American Cities

| Introduction

Bruges, Youngstown, and Boston

In 1301, Philip IV of France and his queen, Joan of Navarra, visited the city of Bruges in their recently acquired territory, Flanders. The lavish entertainment of the royal couple in that city prompted the queen to observe: "I thought that I alone was queen; but here in this place I have 600 rivals" (Dunford, Holland, and Lee 1990, p. 366). In the thirteenth and fourteenth centuries, Flanders and northern Italy were the most urbanized parts of Europe (Nicholas 1997). At the time of the monarchs' visit, Bruges had a population of 40,000, compared with 100,000 in the major Italian cities of the time and 50,000 in London; but Bruges was a prosperous town, producing fine woolen textiles that were exported all over Europe. The chief input, wool, was imported from England. Bruges differed from the other textile manufacturing centers of Flanders (Ghent, Ypres, and Douai) because it was also an international trading hub. It had hosted a major trade fair annually since at least 1200. As overland transport became eclipsed by sea transport at the end of the thirteenth century, Bruges, possessing a seaport, "became the pre-eminent center of international trade in north-western Europe" (Geirnaert and Vandamme 1996, p. 26). Tailors and other skilled craftsmen composed one-fifth of the Bruges work force. Another quarter of its residents were engaged in wholesale trade and finance. Financial services, such as current accounts, money transfers, deposits, short- and long-term loans, and investment capital, were provided to local, regional, and international traders. Trade in letters of exchange, used to settle international monetary transactions, went on at the town square, where the Genoese, Florentine, and Venetian bankers and merchants were located. The square was called the Beursplein, after the Van der Beurse family, who operated a hotel on the square. Thus, the origin of the term *bourse* for a stock exchange was in fourteenth-century Bruges (Geirnaert and Vandamme 1996). Bruges's prosperity rested upon its concentration of human capital in the form of skilled workers and on its role as a center of financial services.

The silting up of Bruges's route to the North Sea, shifts in export demand, the rise of Antwerp and Amsterdam, war, and political conflict betwen France and England, all changed Bruges's fortunes. In 1452, an Italian living in Bruges referred to the city as "a living grave." "By 1494, Bruges found itself impoverished and depopulated. Between four and five thousand houses stood empty" (Geirnaert and Vandamme 1996, p. 45).

Bruges is the medieval version of the American Rustbelt city. On the occasion of the opening of the St. Lawrence Seaway, linking the Great Lakes to the Atlantic Ocean, *National Geographic* published a paean to the industrial cities of the heartland of the United States (Kenney 1959). A golden future was envisioned at the time, but many of those industrial cities have not fared well. Youngstown, Ohio, for example, highly specialized in steel production, has suffered from the long decline in that industry.

An established center of iron production after the Civil War (1860–65), Youngstown converted to steel manufacturing in the 1890s. The Youngstown Iron Sheet and Tube Company was created by local investors in 1900. It entered the exploding market for steel sheet, tinplate, and pipe used for tin cans, autos, and pipes for the booming oil fields of the southwest. In 1900 the population of Youngstown, Ohio, was 45,000. Thirty years later it was 170,000, making Youngstown 43rd in size among U.S. cities. "This fourfold multiplication of people resulted from the rise of the steel industry in the first decades of the twentieth century" (Blue et al. 1995, p. 93). Immigrants flooded into Youngstown from eastern and southern Europe to work in the steel mills.

The lowest-cost means of transporting the heavy inputs and outputs of steel mills was by water, and in that respect Youngstown was at a disadvantage with its competitors in Pittsburgh, Cleveland, and Gary. Youngstown producers used rail while the others used water. However, "its rolling mills were able to charge prices that covered these expenses because of great demand" (Blue et al. 1995,

p. 94). Local interests pressed Congress to build a canal linking Youngstown with the Ohio River, and thus all of the industrial heartland, but to no avail. Despite that transport disadvantage, by mid-century Youngstown was the fourth largest center of steel production in the United States. World War II and the postwar boom greatly increased the demand for steel, and that brought prosperity to Youngstown. Youngstown was living the American dream.

The dream vanished. Because of the transport-cost disadvantage, steel producers did not reinvest in Youngstown. Faced with increased competition from foreign producers, the United States' steel production stagnated. The modernization of facilities that was required to be competitive came late and was concentrated on plants in other places, places with better transport than Youngstown had. A laid-off steel worker of the Ohio Works in Youngstown complained to a journalist, "The mill is run by a steam engine built in 1908. It's very crude. Whenever something breaks, we make the part. They never buy anything. When you walk in there you step back to 1913" (Maharidge 1985, p. 22).

The Youngstown economy has stagnated since about 1969. Population of the metropolitan area that year reached 640,000, which was 21% above 1950's population. Although national employment has expanded 67% since 1969, Youngstown's employment is only 14% higher. Per capita personal income was only 3% below the national average in 1969, but now it is 13% lower. The average real wage in Youngstown is 13% lower than it was in 1969, and population is down 7%. The decline of Youngstown, like the decline of Bruges, was the result of external forces. Unlike Bruges, Youngstown has not yet recovered. Today Bruges is a tourist attraction. With its canals and quaint old buildings it is promoted as the "Venice of the north." Housing in the old city has been snapped up as second homes for well-to-do managers and professional workers from Brussels. Youngstown has been less fortunate. Corrections Corporation of America opened a for-profit prison in Youngstown in 1997, housing 1,700 prisoners imported from the District of Columbia. The company announced in 1999 that it wanted to expand the existing prison by 500 beds and build two more prisons nearby with additional capacity of 5,000 inmates (Yeoman 2000). That is not the industry most mayors would seek to attract.

The Boston metropolitan economy, which accounts for over 80% of Massachusetts' employment, crashed three times during the twentieth century (in addition to cyclical downturns) and has rebounded three times (Castells and Hall

Table I.1. Massachusetts Net Migration, Domestic and International, 1990–1999

Fiscal Year	Net Migration	Net Domestic Migration	Net International Migration
1990/91	−56,196	−69,784	13,588
1991/92	−36,839	−52,925	16,086
1992/93	−11,988	−29,591	17,603
1993/94	−6,823	−22,961	16,138
1994/95	6,367	−11,736	18,103
1995/96	9	−16,652	16,661
1996/97	6,140	−9,775	15,915
1997/98	4,389	−10,077	14,466
1998/99	6,283	−8,656	14,939

Source: U.S. Census Bureau 2000.

1994). At the end of the most recent crash, 1987–90, two economists wrote: "We would forecast that Massachusetts would return to normal [relative employment growth well below the nation] over the next half-decade through a steady increase in net outmigration of workers" (Blanchard and Katz 1992, p. 53).

They were mostly wrong, but partly right. From 1991 through 1996, relative employment growth in Massachusetts almost matched the strong national growth (1.8% versus 1.9% per year). For Boston the relative employment growth, 2.0% per year, was slightly better than that for the nation. The economists were partly right because cumulative net migration for Massachusetts was negative (an outflow) in the five years following their forecast (see Table I.1). But rather than "a steady increase in net outmigration of workers" there has been a steady decrease. As shown above, the biggest outflow, −56,000, occurred in the year before their forecast, 1990–91. In the next three years the outflow became successively smaller, as domestic net migration (negative) lessened, while international net migration (positive) remained steady. Indeed, net migration shifted to positive (inflow) from 1994–95 forward. Boston, like the rest if Massachusetts, has higher employment now than before the economic decline. The city has rebounded from its 1987–90 crash with a high-wage and low-unemployment metropolitan economy.

In their recent book, *The Boston Renaissance*, Bluestone and Stevenson note, "In the half-century since World War II, the Boston region has been transformed from a mill-based to a mind-based economy. . . . The growth of services has eclipsed manufacturing growth" (pp. 12–13).

In Boston, 31% of the adults have college degrees or postgraduate degrees, while in Youngstown 13% do. That difference, I believe, in part explains why Boston has rebounded and Youngstown has not. In Boston, per capita proprietor's income (one crude indicator of entrepreneurial activity) is 12% above the national average. In Youngstown, it is 47% below the national average. Boston has a postindustrial metropolitan economy that is highly specialized in the information sector. Youngstown does not.

Major Themes

In this book I demonstrate the preeminent role of the information sector in the United States economy and the concentration of that sector in large metropolitan areas. The information sector is the fastest growing part of the economy, and it is now as large as the goods production and distribution sector.

One manifestation of the rise of the information sector is its increased prominence in foreign trade. As first the agriculture and raw materials sector and then the manufacturing sector diminish in relative size in the economy, the export of merchandise will of course also diminish in relative importance. What has been rising in relative and absolute importance in foreign trade of the United States is the export of information-sector services, including royalties and license fees. Those information-sector exports were $133 billion in 1999, more than two-thirds of the $193 billion in high-tech exports of computers, semiconductors, aircraft, telecommunication equipment, and scientific instruments, and far larger than agricultural exports, which totaled $50 billion (Bureau of Economic Analysis [hereafter BEA] 2000b).

Economic research in the past two decades has established that nothing improves a person's lifetime earnings as much as higher education (Ehrenberg and Smith 2000). And the new endogenous growth theory in economics argues that a nation's economic growth is promoted as much, if not more, by educational attainment as by capital accumulation. A critical mass of college-educated workers is necessary for developing and sustaining the information sector. Of course, educational requirements have been ratcheted upward in all sectors, but they are markedly high in the information sector.

Jane Jacobs' first book, *The Death and Life of Great American Cities* (1961), has had a profound positive effect on the planning profession. Her later works on urban economies have had a belated impact on urban economists. Her message there is that specialization of an urban economy is bad for growth, diversity is good. That is contrary to the traditional idea in economics that originated with Alfred Marshall in the nineteenth century. A number of economists have recently tested her hypothesis and concluded that she is right. A major proposition of this book is that she is wrong and so are they. Places that are specialized in some traded good or service activity tend to have stronger economies than places without any specialization. Some specializations are better than others and some can be worse than having no specialization, that is, diversity. Not all specializations are good for all time periods. Youngstown had the right specialization, steel production, in 1900, and it became a boomtown. Youngstown had the wrong specialization, steel production, in 1969, and it crashed and has not yet recovered. It is now becoming specialized in prisons, which may be just right if the war on drugs heats up. Houston and other metropolitan areas of the oil patch states are specialized in energy production, and they had stellar economic performance during the energy crisis of the 1970s. They crashed along with oil prices in the 1980s. Fortunately for Houston, it is also specialized in producer services. Boston is specialized in finance and other producer services, and by my criteria almost specialized in higher education and health services, as is New York. They both have strong economies. Norfolk–Newport News is not specialized in anything now that the Cold War has ended, and it has a weak economy. That might change with the war on terrorism. Of the 46 metropolitan areas with populations over one million, only eight have no specialization as defined in this book.

What does specialization have to do with the information sector? It is not a separate theme. I define six groups of traded goods and services industries and argue that the traded goods and services industries are the engines that propel metropolitan economies. Three of them produce or distribute traded *goods*. That set is labeled the goods production and distribution sector. The other three produce traded *services*. That set is labeled the information sector. The label is not arbitrary, as I make clear. Other than the distinction of producing traded services rather than producing and distributing traded goods, the information sector is very different from the goods production and distribution sector. First, the occupational mix of the information sector has far higher proportions of professional, technical, and managerial jobs that pay high wages, and so human capital in the form of workers with higher education is much more important as an input for the information sector than it is for the goods production and distribution sector. But also, the information sector has far higher proportions of clerical and service jobs that pay low wages.

Second, although nationally the information sector is now about the same size as the goods production and distribution sector, it is much larger in all metropolitan territories than the goods production and distribution sector, which is more dispersed and found more in nonmetropolitan territories. Thirty years ago that was not the case. Goods production and distribution dominated metropolitan economies as well as the national economy. Not only is the information sector more concentrated in metropolitan areas but also it tends to be concentrated in the largest metropolitan areas. That suggests that economies gained from spatial concentration, such as knowledge spillovers, are greater for information sector firms than for goods production and distribution firms.

Lest the knowledgeable reader sigh and reply that we have known for decades that the service sector has become bigger than the goods production sector, I must emphasize that my definition of the information sector does *not* include all services. It includes only traded services, that is, services that may be significant sources of revenue from outside the metropolitan area, or significant sources of imports from outside. Further, the two sectors of information and goods production and distribution as defined here do not sum to the entire economy. Excluded are nontraded goods and services such as retail trade, utilities, construction, personal services, and government. True, in some places retail trade is a significant source of outside revenue (Las Vegas and Orlando), as is government (Washington, D.C., and state capitals), but in most metropolitan areas those activities are nontraded.

Metropolitan economies are neither microcosms of the national economy nor cookie-cutter versions of each other at different scales, in terms of their traded goods and services. Two-thirds of all metropolitan areas are specialized, as defined here, and one-third of them are diversified. The specialized places differ from the diversified places and from each other on a number of key characteristics: size, per capita income, and human capital. For economic growth, some specializations help and some hurt. With qualifications saved for later, in the last third of the twentieth century, specialization in the information sector helped metropolitan growth while specialization in the goods production and distribution sector hurt growth.

Twenty years ago, Alvin Toffler proclaimed that the information age was making big cities redundant, anachronisms of a vanishing era. When he wrote that (*The Third Wave*, 1980) there was no Internet or e-mail and there were no fax machines. The same futurist hype continues to be published. More recent examples of the genre are cited by Gaspar and Glaeser (1998) "Roger Naisbitt (1995), Nicholas Negroponte (1995), and William Knobe (1996) are among the many prognosticators who have weighed in on this topic and generally forecast the end of the need for cities. . . . These seers assert that electronics will eliminate the need for face-to-face interactions and the cities which facilitate those interactions" (Gaspar and Glaeser 1998, pp. 136–137). In the same vein but less extreme, in a recent report the Office of Technology Assessment (1995) of the U.S. Congress asserted that computer and communication technology was lessening the attachment of information jobs to metropolitan locations, making them much more footloose. I believe the opposite to be the case: expansion of the information sector is accompanied by *greater* concentration of that sector in large metropolitan areas, despite the proliferation of distance-eliminating technologies. Simultaneously, relative contraction of the manufacturing sector is accompanied by greater dispersion of manufacturing in smaller metropolitan areas and outside of metropolitan areas altogether, a process perhaps abetted by those technologies.

Economists who write about economic growth focus upon a convenient abstraction created by macroeconomics, the national economy. The national economy is a collection of averages and aggregations which conceals much too much. Economic growth, as is well appreciated, does not proceed smoothly over time. But neither does it proceed smoothly over space, over rural and metropolitan space, even over different metropolitan places. Boston's real per capita income has grown 67% since 1969, Youngstown's has grown 39%, and the national average has grown 49%. Metropolitan economies that are specialized in some parts of the information sector are more likely to have higher per capita income and stronger growth than metropolitan economies with traditional specializations in manufacturing or distribution. The disparate fortunes of American metropolitan areas and their central cities are *not* explained by the old Snowbelt-Sunbelt dichotomy of Kirkpatrick Sale (1975) nor by the "elastic-inelastic" framework of David Rusk's *Cities Without Suburbs* (1995). To elaborate on this proposition a bit, for about one hundred years or so, some economists have noted that in the development of industrialized nations, there is an evolution of dominant and receding economic sectors. Agriculture and primary products (forestry, fisheries, and mines) form the dominant sector on the eve of industrialization. Then the goods production sector (manufacturing and construction) becomes dominant, as in the United States from the end of the Civil War through the first half of the twentieth century. Then distribution (transportation, utilities, and trade), the tertiary sector, becomes dominant; and finally, in my scheme, the information sector (producer services and advanced consumer services) approaches dominance. Because it is the fastest growing sector of the U.S. economy, metropolitan areas that are more specialized in the information sector or are *becoming* more specialized in the information sector experience stronger economic growth and higher levels of prosperity than places frozen in specializations of the past.

A related proposition is that losing factory jobs in big cities need not be a permanent disaster for the minority population in those cities if the local economy evolves in the right direction. It may be true that some of the beneficiaries of the transformation from a manufacturing economy to an information economy are the lower income minority populations of metropolitan areas undergoing such a transformation. William Julius Wilson's sad story (*The Truly Disadvantaged*, 1987) about blacks in northern cities being left jobless and downwardly mobile as factory jobs disappeared to the suburbs, South Carolina, and South Korea is a story about manufacturing economies in Midwestern cities stuck in specializations of the past. Philadelphia is not one of those places, but Detroit is. In the booming 1980s, median income of black households in Philadelphia proper rose 31%, adjusted for inflation, and the number of black residents in high-poverty neighborhoods declined 20%. In Detroit such incomes fell 19% and the black population in poverty neighborhoods jumped up 246%, surpassing Chicago and making Detroit second only to New York in the number of black residents in high-poverty neighborhoods. The Chicago number doubled in the 1970s, when it was hemorrhaging manufacturing jobs, and then hardly budged from 1980 to 1990 (Jargowsky 1997). Philadelphia and Chicago have become specialized in the information sector. Detroit has not. The left-liberal and right-populist hostility to a "yuppie" economy flows from the same perception: an economy dominated by the information sector does nothing or less for blacks or for less-skilled workers. They may be wrong. Boston, like New York and San Francisco, is highly specialized in the information sector, that is, a "yuppie" economy. Yet black households' real income in Boston rose 40% in the 1980s, faster than in any other of the 50 largest cities, and faster than the national rise in all households' income of only 7% in the 1980s (Drennan, Tobier, and Lewis 1996). But they may be right, and we will not know for sure until the 2000 census provides current solid data on incomes and poverty in metropolitan areas and their central cities.

If metropolitan areas specialized in the information sector tend to be larger, with higher per capita incomes, more human capital, and better economic growth, then are smaller places with opposite characteristics falling behind? According to economic theory, per capita incomes of regions, states, and metropolitan areas do converge in the long-run. That is because higher wages in places where labor is relatively scarce will attract labor from places where wages are low and labor is relatively abundant. So wages will move closer together as labor flows out of low-wage places and into high-wage places. The same argument applies to capital. Numerous studies in economics have tested that hypothesis for nations and for parts of the United States: regions, states, and metropolitan areas. For nations the evidence is mixed, for parts of the United States the evidence mostly supported convergence, until ten years ago. A number of researchers found evidence of dispersion, the opposite of convergence, for states and metropolitan areas in the 1980s. Others dismissed that evidence of dispersion as the result of short-term aberrations. José Lobo and I have shown that the metropolitan dispersion during the 1980s has continued into the 1990s (Drennan and Lobo 1999 and forthcoming). One theme in this book is that the observed dispersion of metropolitan incomes is tied to size, specialization, and human capital. In 1990, the Nobel laureate in economics, Robert Lucas, noted that if the theory of convergence were correct, capital would be pouring into India, where it is relatively scarce, but of course it is not (Lucas 1990). Some factors that the theory has overlooked must be at work. In that vein I must note that the studies of convergence among nations tend to support convergence among the rich nations, but not among rich nations and poor nations, like India. Following Lucas, I observe that human capital is relatively abundant in Boston and relatively scarce in Youngstown. Yet there has been no stampede of the well-educated from Boston to Youngstown or to other educationally challenged metropolitan areas. Unlike the case of India, where different currency, customs, and laws all present barriers to capital flows from rich nations, there are no such barriers between Boston and Youngstown. Clearly the returns to human capital in Boston must be better than in Youngstown, despite the relative abundance of human capital in Boston, as any recent MBA graduate could tell you. It may be true in a modern economy that the returns to human capital are enhanced, not diminished, in places with an abundant supply (Rauch 1993). I think that metropolitan income divergence will stay with us for some time. Has that ever happened before? In his fascinating book, *The Wealth and Poverty of Nations: Why Some Are So Rich and Some Are So Poor,* Landes notes that "in 1750s the difference between western Europe (excluding Britain) and eastern in income per head was perhaps 15%; in 1800 little more than 20. By 1860 it was up to 64%; by the 1900s almost 80%" (Landes 1998, p. 194).

Those are the major themes in this book. They have policy implications for all levels of government. If it is true that: (1) the information sector is the fastest growing part of the economy, and (2) it is the most competitive sector we have in world trade, and (3) it has become more concentrated in our largest metropolitan areas, and (4) it critically depends on attracting a well-educated work force while at the same time, perhaps, expanding jobs and incomes for less-skilled populations in cities, then all levels of government should pay more attention to public sector steps to foster its flourishing. There are cost-effective actions that the federal government could pursue which would help the information sector to thrive in large cities. There are actions which state governments could pursue to promote the flourishing of the information sector in large cities, which would promote broader job and income growth there. Of course there are policies big city mayors could pursue, too, which would encourage expansion of the information sector and thus contribute to broader economic growth.

Outline of Chapters

In Chapter 1, I define the information sector in a concrete fashion, so that published data can be used to measure that sector and compare it with the other major parts of the economy over time. One could quarrel with my definition as including too much or excluding too much, but that would not be an interesting quarrel. I am certain that my definition encompasses the essential core of the information sector. Some brief intellectual history of the idea of the information sector is presented, because it is certainly not new with this book. The occupational structure of the information sector is described and compared with other parts of the economy in order to show that it is far more top-heavy with highly educated workers than other sectors.

In the second chapter, I analyze gross product, employment, and earnings in the information sector over time and compare those data with the other traded goods and services sector, goods production and distribution (which includes manufacturing, mining, agriculture, transportation, and wholesale trade). The data show that the information sector has grown much faster than the other sector and that the two are now about equal in size. Intersector flows of inputs and outputs for a few points in time, derived from input-output tables, enable me to show the changing relationships among the sectors over time. Perhaps the most interesting change is that the information sector consumes more inputs from manufacturing than vice versa. I next note the rising importance of information sector corporations compared with industrial corporations. The international dimension of the U.S. information sector is described, namely trade in the information sector's output, foreign direct investment by U.S. information sector firms, and the aggressive international expansion of such firms. Finally, I compare the stock market performance of information sector firms with that of goods production and distribution firms over the 2000–2001 stock market decline that wiped out so many "new economy" firms, even before the destruction of the World Trade Center brought on a further stock market drop.

In Chapters 1 and 2, all of the data that I present relate to the United States economy. In Chapter 3 I shift the focus to metropolitan economies. There I link the sectoral evolution of the national economy to the shifting economic fortunes of all the metropolitan economies. Metropolitan areas are sorted into types based upon their economic specialization or absence of specialization. The places so classified and their numbers change over time. Characteristics of sets of places with different specializations are compared for different time periods. The issues of agglomeration economies, human capital, and urban size and growth are described in the context of economic specialization, particularly specialization in the information sector. Almost all large metropolitan areas (i.e., with population more than one million) have been increasing in population over the past several decades. That has not been the case with their central cities. In the final part of Chapter 3, the large metropolitan areas with growing central cities, 1990–2000, are compared with those with declining central cities to determine if they differ with respect to specialization. The question of interest is whether large metropolitan areas with rising city population are more likely to be specialized in the information sector than large metropolitan areas with declining city population.

The descriptive data of Chapter 3 suggest testable propositions regarding the importance of specialization, urban size, and human capital in determining metropolitan income levels and growth as well as in determining metropolitan population and employment growth. In Chapter 4, I estimate models for testing those propositions, evaluate the results, and use some of the estimated equations to calculate the impacts of individual variables upon metropolitan income levels and upon growth of income, population, and employment.

In Chapter 5 I address the question of metropolitan income convergence. The data that I developed with José Lobo (Drennan and Lobo forthcoming) are presented, showing a clear pattern of divergence beginning in the mid-1970s. In light of those results, I sort out two groups of places from all metropolitan places. The first is the set that diverged *up* over the past quarter-century (initial income above average and subsequent growth above average). The second is the set that diverged *down* (initial incomes below average and subsequent growth below average). I then compare the sets of places in terms of size, specialization or its absence, and levels of human capital. The interesting fact that some places are surging ahead while many are lagging behind over such a long period begs the question What does it all mean for the distribution of household income in metropolitan areas, for low-income households, for minority households, in places doing well compared with those not doing well? There are two obvious questions that should be addressed. First, do metropolitan economies specialized in the information sector have higher or lower rates of city poverty than places specialized in goods production and distribution and than places with no specialization? Second, is the distribution of household income better (i.e., smaller proportions of households in the bottom income classes) or worse in places specialized in the information sector than in the other types of places? In Chapter 5 I do address the question about city poverty rates. Unfortunately, I cannot address the second question, because the available evidence is either too old (1990 decennial census) or too sparse. The jury may be out on that issue until the 2000 census data on income distribution are released.

Finally in Chapter 6, I draw conclusions and point to implications of the earlier chapters for what would be sound public policies (i.e., promoting of metropolitan economic growth and income enhancement) for federal, state, and local governments. I think the most important implication is that the federal government should abandon its laissez-faire stance on the construction and access pricing of the fiber-optic network that private firms were furiously building before the crash of high-tech stocks.

I have tried to keep the text as uncluttered as possible with statistical tables and equations. What tables or charts do appear are terse and to the point. A cornucopia of tables is available on line as a supplement to this text, at www .press.jhu.edu/press/books/titles/s02/s02drin.htm and at www.crp.cornell.edu/ publications/facultypubs/drennan/Supplement_list.html.

1 | Describing the Elephant
The Information Sector

In the mid-1960s, there were more than 850,000 manufacturing and mining employees in New York City, of which 100,000 were office workers in Manhattan. Many of those office workers were employed by the 128 *Fortune* 500 industrial corporations with headquarters in the city. A large sample of premium midtown office space for that period revealed that 45% was occupied by manufacturing and mining corporations while only 10% was occupied by financial and law firms (Conservation of Human Resources 1977). In the intervening years, manufacturing and mining employment in New York City has fallen to 260,000, of which only 29,000 represent office jobs in Manhattan. The number of *Fortune* 500 industrial corporations with headquarters in Manhattan has dropped to 30. Yet grass is not growing in the streets. The stock of Manhattan office space is roughly 50% greater than it was in the mid-1960s, the vacancy rate is lower, and real office rents are higher. The information sector has displaced the industrial corporations and now occupies most of the Manhattan office space, especially the premium space. Financial firms and law firms together take one-half of the space (*New York Times* 2000). The story of one building encapsulates that sea change. In 1969 when General Motors moved into its signature office tower on Fifth Avenue across from the Plaza Hotel, it occupied half of the 50 floors. When it sold the building in 1991, it occupied only three floors plus a showroom. The transformation of the Manhattan office economy mirrors the transformation of the national economy and its metropolitan areas.

Defining the Information Sector

What I call the information sector can be split into three groups of industries, two that deal in producer services and one providing advanced consumer services. The first is financial producer services, which includes the industries of banking, securities, insurance, and real estate. The second group is other producer services, which includes the industries of communication (telephone, television, and radio), business, professional, and legal services. Economic activities classified within business services (Standard Industrial Classification [SIC] code 73) include computer software and data services, advertising, public relations, commercial research, temporary help agencies, equipment rental, protection services, and services to buildings. Professional services (SIC 87) include engineering, architecture, accounting, and management consulting.

The two groups of producer services are services provided to business, to government, and to nonprofit organizations. A considerable body of literature on producer services has been published over the past 25 years by researchers in geography and in urban and regional studies. The original concept of identifying those particular industries with knowledge and information is older. In his major work, *Megalopolis,* the geographer Jean Gottmann (1961) coined the phrase *quaternary sector* to distinguish a fourth grouping of economic activities, those which intensively used and produced information. Gottmann argued that the traditional three sectors (primary, secondary, and tertiary) failed to capture all economic activities.

In 1962, the economist most noted for his work on risk and investment, Fritz Machlup, published *The Production and Distribution of Knowledge in the United States.* That work drew the attention of economists to the importance of knowledge or information in a modern economy. The producer service literature of the past 25 years, however, has flourished outside of mainstream economics, mainly in geography, regional science, and urban political economy. The major bibliographical journal in economics, *The Journal of Economic Literature,* has never published a review piece on the producer service literature.

Producer services, financial and other, are information-intensive industries in which much of the output is intermediate rather than final (Noyelle and Stanback 1984; Coffey and Polese 1989). The producer service output is often customized, and its production utilizes a highly skilled white-collar work force of managers, professionals, and technical workers along with large numbers of less-skilled clerical workers (Beyers 1992). The producer service industries are a subset of what Machlup (1962) called knowledge-producing industries, and what Porat (1977) labeled the primary information sector. The definition of producer services that I use in this study corresponds very closely to those used in previous studies in the producer services literature (Noyelle and Stanback 1984; Baumol, Osberg, and Wolff 1989; Beyers 1992; Drennan 1992; Drennan, Tobier, and Lewis 1996; Drennan 1999). Some studies have excluded the finance, insurance, and real estate industries from producer services (Hansen 1990; Esparza and Krmenec 1996). Few studies include communication as a producer service industry (Noyelle and Peace 1991; Drennan 1999). Finance, insurance, real estate, and communications are defined as producer services in this book because a large part of their output is intermediate input for other industries, rather than final demand, as shown in the latest input-output tables for the United States. In the producer services industries included here, output for intermediate use as a percent of total output ranges from 40% (computer and data processing services) to 99% (advertising). The share in finance is 45% and in communications it is 48% (BEA 2000a). The list of industries included in the two producer services groups and their Standard Industrial Classification codes are in the Appendix.

The third group of industries composing the information sector, advanced consumer services, is here defined as high-level services provided to consumers. Like producer services, they are mostly nonroutine, they tend to have a high information content, and they tend to be provided by a highly skilled professional work force. Unlike producer services, there is not an extensive scholarly literature on the group of industries that I call advanced consumer services. Like producer services, advanced consumer services intensively use information or knowledge. Unlike producer services, almost all of their output is for final demand. There are studies of individual parts of the advanced consumer services sector, such as the huge health care industry. No study analyzes the rising importance of this collection of industries in the national economy or its impact upon metropolitan economies. Everyone knows that the growth of Las Vegas and Orlando are linked to the amusement industry, a part of advanced consumer services. Not as obvious are the impacts of universities and the health care industry upon numerous urban areas.

Advanced consumer service industries include professional sports, music, theater, motion picture production, museums, private health services, and private education at all levels. Note that not all services to consumers are included in my advanced consumer services part of the information sector. Auto repair, hair styling, dry cleaning, laundries, hotels, health clubs, and social services among others are excluded because they are not information intensive, they tend to require a less-skilled work force, and their output tends to be routine rather than specialized. Another reason, to be explained in Chapter 2, is that those excluded services are not traded services. The list of advanced consumer service industries and their SIC codes is in the Appendix.

The criterion for inclusion in one of the two producer service groups or in the advanced consumer service group is that the activity be information intensive. Not all services are information intensive. The characteristics of information-intensive industries are that the output is often nonhomogeneous, the output may be information, information may be a central input, and the occupational structure includes a high proportion of managers, professional, and technical workers.

A word about the definitions of the industries I have included (listed in the Appendix). I have chosen industries by two-digit SIC code as the basic building blocks for my definition, when in fact three and four digit SIC industries would enable me to make finer distinctions and thus zero in on what are truly information-intensive economic activities. But the data set which I use for the analysis of metropolitan areas, an analysis so central to my arguments, is not available on a more detailed basis than two-digit SIC industries. I have sacrificed greater precision in the operational definition in order to tell the interesting story about the information sector in metropolitan economies. A few examples of what is lost. One of the advanced consumer service industries is motion pictures, SIC code 78. It includes motion picture production, which is certainly an information-intensive activity, and motion picture exhibition, which is certainly not. One of the largest producer service industries is business services (SIC 73). It includes computer and data processing services, advertising, commercial art, and news syndicates, all of which are information-intensive activities. But business services also includes cleaning and window washing services to office buildings, private protection services, and equipment rental services, none of which could be described as information-intensive activities. Excluded from my set of industries which compose the information sector is the manufacturing industry printing and publishing (SIC code 27). Within that industry are newspaper, periodical, and book publishing, all of which are information-intensive activities. But because they are lumped together with the printing industries, they are excluded from my operational definition of the information sector. The most significant exclusion is that state universities and colleges and government-run hospitals are not included in advanced consumer services as they should be. The available data for metropolitan areas aggregates public higher education and public hospitals with all government. The size of the advanced consumer services part of the information sector is thus understated.

In addition to inappropriate exclusions and inclusions from the information sector, forced by the limited availability of metropolitan data, at least one part is in the wrong group. Communication (SIC 48) includes telephone service and television and radio broadcasting. Television and radio clearly belong in advanced consumer services, while telephone service belongs in other producer services. But because the separate parts of the communication industry are not published for metropolitan areas, the entire industry is included in other producer services.

The inadequacy of the Standard Industrial Classification system for capturing the burgeoning information economy has finally been recognized by the federal government. A new system, the North American Industrial Classification System will gradually replace the SIC system over the next few years, but far too late for this book.

Intellectual Origin of the Information Sector

There are two separate but overlapping intellectual strands that lead up to my analysis of the information sector. The first is the evolutionary view of an economy in which all economic activity is partitioned into two or more sectors. The primary sector—agriculture, forestry, fisheries, and mining—engages most of the work force in a preindustrial era. With industrialization, relatively more labor and capital shift into the secondary sector of manufacturing and construction. Then, with time, the tertiary sector, transportation and trade, becomes relatively more important than it was in the early era of industrialization. Finally the service sector, or quaternary sector or information sector, becomes relatively large. There is a dynamic feedback whereby each new sector's emergence contributes to the productivity of the older sectors. The output of manufacturers—tractors, reapers, chain saws, trucks, marine engines—enhanced the efficiency of agriculture, forestry, and fisheries. The development and expansion of shipping, railroads, air freight, wholesaling, and retailing has increased the markets for both manufactured goods and primary products. The volume of Chilean fruit and vegetable production has expanded with transportation improvements that opened North American markets in winter. The proliferation of multinational manufacturing corporations has been stimulated and facilitated by the development of foreign exchange markets, sophisticated risk management, and capital markets that are truly international. Indeed, the commodities futures markets in Chicago, New York, and London make agriculture less risky and therefore more efficient than in the past. Thus, newer sectors contribute to the productivity of older sectors.

This evolutionary view may first have been stated in simple form by Sir James Steuart in 1767, as reported by Beckmann (1981). A number of economists have developed the evolutionary view, and the first to do so after Steuart was Haig (1926), followed by Fisher (1935). Colin Clark, an English economist most noted for development of national income accounting concepts, elaborated the evolutionary view in his book, *The Conditions of Economic Progress* (1951). The French geographer Jean Gottmann was the first writer to add a fourth sector, naming it quaternary, as noted above. Beckmann (1981) added to that literature, and recently the evolutionary process of sectoral relative growth among nations was described in an International Monetary Fund paper (Rowthorn and Ramaswamy 1997). But most significant has been the contribution of Herbert Simon (1947, 1982), who developed a formal model that "demonstrated how increasing economic productivity would lead inexorably to changes in the structure of the economy and the spatial distribution of activities and population" (Jones 1984). In the Simon model the economy is split into two sectors, rural and urban. The rural sector, located in the rural area, produces an agricultural commodity. The urban sector, located in the urban area, produces an urban commodity. Total population and employment are assumed to be fixed. The driving force in the Simon model is technological change, which raises productivity (output per worker) at the same rate in both sectors and thus raises real incomes. Simon assumes that demand for the urban good is more sensitive to increases in income, that is, is more income elastic, than is demand for the rural good. As incomes rise over time, there will be a relative shift of output and employment out of the rural good and into the urban good. Given that the rural good production is located in the rural area and the urban good production is not, then, over time, employment and population will shift out of the rural area and into the urban area. All developed nations have had a long-term shift of population from rural areas into urban areas, and the Simon model explains the observed shift.

Simon did not test his model, but Barclay Jones tested it for the United States (1984). Jones recast the Simon model within the evolutionary view of long-term economic development by moving from Simon's two sectors, rural and urban, to four sectors. His four sectors correspond to the traditional industry taxonomy of the evolutionary view of economic development. They are primary (agriculture, forestry, fisheries, and mining), secondary (manufacturing and construction), tertiary (transportation, utilities, and trade), and services (communication, finance, insurance, real estate, services, and government). What Jones labels "services" Gottmann (1961) labeled "quaternary." They are not quite the same. Jones follows the broad categories employed in government reporting of economic statistics for industries whereas Gottmann had in mind a conceptual difference between the quaternary sector and all others. That difference is the central importance of information as both an input and an output for the quaternary sector. The government's classification scheme does not sort activities on that difference. Gas stations and hardware stores are part of retail trade and therefore are in the tertiary sector as traditionally defined. Laundromats and auto repair shops are part of services, trash collection is part of government and they are all therefore in the services sector as traditionally defined and used by Jones. But from the conceptual perspective that Gottmann had in mind, there is no distinction among all those activities based on the importance of information as an input or output. For my purposes here, the traditional classification scheme employed by Jones is not adequate.

Although Simon was seeking to explain the observed shift of population and employment from rural to urban places, he made no distinction among types of urban places. I believe that Jones's paper (1984) includes the first explicit inference that the spatial impact of evolving national sectors growing at different rates would result in shifts in both the number and the size of urban areas of different types. He speculates that the relative rise of his fourth sector, services, favors urban areas that are central places (i.e., specializing in services for a wide hinterland of smaller places and rural areas) and are amenity-rich places.

In a similar vein, Henderson (1988) developed a far more elaborate model that seeks to explain both the number and the size of urban areas of different types. The types are defined in terms of specialization in different traded goods. Traded goods are those which can be exported from and imported to an urban area. In Henderson's model, long-term changes in the composition of national demand, changes in productivity, and changes in scale economies among the different traded goods industries result in shifts in the number and size of urban areas of different types. That is an extraordinary idea, linking as it does secular changes in the national economy to the composition of the urban hierarchy. Although I believe Jones (1984) expressed that idea first, it is Henderson who developed it rigorously. Henderson argues that as the composition of national demand shifts, the numbers of urban places specialized in production of each component of that national demand will change accordingly. That is, for example, if durable manufactured goods diminish in relative importance in national demand, then the relative number of urban places specialized in the production of durable goods will also decline. He also argues that differential productivity growth across sectors has an impact upon the mix of urban places. For example, if relative productivity (output per worker) rises in durable manufacturing, then the relative number of urban places specialized in durable manufacturing will decline. In a recent paper (1999), I tested those propositions of Henderson's and found support for them.

There are two problems with Henderson's approach. First, he focused almost exclusively upon traded *goods,* not services, which is a bias typical of economists. Second, his concept of specialization is very narrow. Rather than the four exhaustive sectors of Jones (1984), Henderson identifies about one dozen subparts of manufacturing as the traded goods specializations. Note that in this first intellectual strand that I call sector evolution, there is no explicit identification of an information sector except by the geographer Gottmann (1961).

The second intellectual strand focuses on the idea of an information sector, although not always with that name. One of the first economic studies in that area was Machlup's *The Production and Distribution of Knowledge in the United States* (1962). The famous book by the sociologist Daniel Bell, *The Coming of Post-Industrial Society* (1973), placed the idea of an information economy in the heads of a wide audience. The most comprehensive attempt to define precisely and to measure the information sector is the multivolume work by M. Porat, *The Information Economy: Definition and Measurement* (1977). None of those works or the more theoretical economic works on information and knowledge (Arrow 1962; Stigler 1961) join the idea of an information sector with that of the urban space economy. The geographer Allan Pred may be one of the first writers to make that link, in his book *City Systems in Advanced Economies* (1977). There he cogently argues that workers in information industries, such as financial services and advertising, spend much of their time processing and exchanging information that is not routine. Therefore, their efficiency is enhanced by concentration in space with other information workers, not necessarily of the same organization. Pred also pointed out that, in a modern economy dominated by firms with activity in multiple locations, impulses of economic growth or decline are transmitted from the place where decisions are made, the firm headquarters, to places where the firm's operations are located. In such a modern economy, the magnitude of the growth or decline impulse is not at all directly tied to distance between the decision center and the location of an operating unit.

The significance of the rise of the information sector for one urban area, New York City, is laid out in *The Corporate Headquarters Complex in New York City* (Conservation of Human Resources 1977), a study that I did with Robert Cohen. From the late 1970s to the present, there has been a great deal of work on the larger subpart of the information sector, producer services. Most of that work has been descriptive and qualitative. The authors of articles and books on producer services include economists (mostly regional and urban), geographers, political scientists, and urban planners. In her book, *The Global City* (1991), Saskia Sassen provides a thorough history of the emergence of a distinct category of producer services. She notes that the term *producer services* as used to describe the information-intensive activities that are mostly services to organizations rather than households was first coined by H. I. Greenfield in his book *Manpower and the Growth of Producer Services* (1966). That was followed by Singlemann's study on sectoral transformation in a set of industrialized countries (1974) and Singlemann and Browning's article on industrial transformation and occupational change (1980). Those works on producer services did not, however, have a spatial dimension. The producer services literature expanded greatly in the 1980s and 1990s, and most of that literature is decidedly spatial in its orientation. The authors cited by Sassen in her review of the producer services literature include Stanback et al. (1981), Daniels (1985), Wood (1987), and Marshall (1986). The book by Noyelle and Stanback, *The Economic Transformation of American Cities* (1984), is probably cited more often than any other work in the subsequent producer services literature. There is a host of other writers who have advanced the analysis of producer services in a spatial context in academic articles and books, including Bailly, Beyers, Coffey, Drennan, Hansen, Isserman, Krmenec, Polese, Schwartz, and Warf. Most of that literature appears in regional science and urban economics journals. The scholar most associated with the rise of an information economy in a spatial context is Manuel Castells, professor of urban planning at Berkeley. His book, *The Informational City* (1989), is a landmark. In that work he addresses the interrelationships between the rise of information technology, restructuring of capitalism, location of high-tech manufacturing, and internationalization of the economy. His more recent book, *The Rise of the Network Society* (1996), is a cogent and highly abstract analysis of the spatial and social implications of the computer and telecommunication revolution in advanced economies.

Occupational Structure of the Information Sector

A social studies text used in the Youngstown elementary schools in the 1950s, *Our Neighbors Tell Us about Their Work* (Aley 1949), is organized around fictitious Youngstown students in a class telling about their parents' jobs. The occupational snapshot that emerges seems extraordinary today. Of the 30 job-holding parents described, only two are women. Four are professionals, and they are all men. Twenty-three of the 30 are men with blue-collar jobs. Whether that accurately reflected the occupational distribution of Youngstown at mid-century is not the point. The point is that that was the *perception* of a normal job mix conveyed to the Youngstown children by the author, an educator in the Youngstown school district. No American city has such a job mix today.

There are seven broad classes of occupations defined by the U.S. Department of Labor. Two of them, managerial and professional, are the occupational classes heavily dominated by people with college degrees or higher education. The three parts of the information sector (financial producer services, other producer services, and advanced consumer services) differ markedly from the other parts of the economy in that they are top-heavy with managerial and professional workers, particularly professional workers. Table 1.1 details the national distribution in 1997. The share of managerial and professional jobs ranged from 31% to 56% in the information sector parts. It ranged from only 14% to 18% in the other parts of the economy. In advanced consumer services, which is dominated by the health and private education industries, 51% of all the jobs were professional. In other producer services, that share was 28%, and in financial producer services it was 18%. None of the other parts of the economy had such large proportions of professional workers. Manufacturing, with a 12% share, ranked above all the other parts outside the information sector.

Among the lowest-skilled, and lowest-paid, of the broad occupational categories is "service workers." The shares of those types of jobs are tiny in the primary production, manufacturing, and distribution sectors (1% to 3% in 1997). Those shares are substantial in parts of the information sector: advanced consumer services (21%) and other producer services (13%). The masses of low-skilled service workers in the health care industry, particularly in hospitals, probably accounts for the unusually high share in advanced consumer services.

The financial producer service industries have the very highest concentration of clerical jobs (47%). The other producer services group ranks second (27%). All the other groups ranged from 9% to 23% in 1997. The relatively high share in financial producer services reflects the job structures of banks and insurance companies.

The three parts of the information sector have the very lowest shares of production worker (i.e., blue-collar) jobs, ranging from 4% to 16%. That is in sharp contrast with manufacturing, where 67% of all jobs were production worker jobs, with distribution (42%), and with the primary production sector of agriculture and mining (31%).

This sector-occupation snapshot for 1997 establishes a number of facts that serve as important background. First, the information sector is quite different in its occupational composition than the other sectors shown. The difference arises from having unusually high shares of professional workers (highly educated and higher paid), clerical workers, and service workers (lower paid), and of course unusually low shares of production workers. Second, the three parts of the information sector differ a good deal among themselves in their occupational composition. Third, there are substantial shares of lower-skilled, lower-paid clerical

Table 1.1. Occupational Distributions within Sectors of U.S. Economy, 1997

(percentages)

Occupation	Goods Production and Distribution			Information			All Other Industries
	Primary Production	Manufacturing	Distribution	Financial Producer Services	Other Producer Services	Advanced Consumer Services	
Managers and administrators	6.1	6.2	7.9	12.6	8.2	5.0	6.2
Professionals	9.8	12.1	6.2	18.3	27.9	51.4	11.5
Sales workers	1.5	3.3	17.0	11.5	6.7	1.9	20.7
Clerical workers	9.5	9.9	23.1	47.5	27.2	15.5	13.3
Service workers	0.8	1.2	2.7	4.7	13.3	21.2	25.6
Agricultural and related	41.2	0.5	1.0	1.2	0.4	0.7	0.8
Production workers	31.1	66.7	42.0	4.2	16.3	4.3	22.0
TOTAL	100.0	100.0	100.0	100.0	100.0	100.0	100.0

Source: U.S. Department of Labor, Bureau of Labor Statistics 1999.

and service jobs in each of the three parts of the information sector. Indeed, the sum of the clerical plus service job shares ranged from 37% in advanced consumer services to 52% in financial producer services. Thus, the information sector not only has unusually high proportions of jobs for college graduates but it also has large proportions of jobs for workers with high school or less education.

2 | Emergence of the Information Sector

In 1993, a man-made flood in Chicago knocked out the power to office towers in the Chicago Loop, shutting them down for a few days. The below-street-level flood reached them all because the buildings are linked by a system of tunnels, built in the early part of the twentieth century. The original purpose of the tunnels was to facilitate the delivery of large volumes of coal to the skyscrapers, essential for heating the huge spaces. A *New York Times* photo of the tunnels after the water was removed revealed their modern use: There was not a trace of coal anywhere. They were lined, virtually packed, with networks of fiber-optic cables, the arteries of the information economy.

Having defined the information sector in a manner that affords unambiguous measurement, we can eschew anecdotes about an amorphous thing variously called the "new economy," the "service economy," the "information economy," the "network society," and the "postindustrial society." In this chapter I present a revised taxonomy of industries, which clearly separates information industries from other service industries.

A Revised Taxonomy of Industries

In the taxonomy of industries utilized in the evolutionary view of an economy, there are four sectors, as in Jones (1984) and as noted in Chapter 1. Those sectors are: (1) primary (agriculture, forestry, fisheries, and mining), (2) secondary (manufacturing and construction), (3) tertiary or distribution (transportation, utilities, and trade), and (4) services (communication, finance, insurance, real estate, services, and government). There are two problems with the traditional taxonomy. The first, as noted, is that it does not group the information-intensive activities into one sector. Rather, they are all in the fourth sector, services, along with many industries that are not information intensive. That is not a trivial issue. As Castells argues,

> To understand the new type of economic and social structure, we must start by characterizing different types of "services" in order to establish clear distinctions between them. In understanding the information economy, each one of the specific categories of services becomes as important a distinction as was the old borderline between manufacturing and services in the preceding type of industrial economy. As economies become more complex, we must diversify the concepts through which we categorize economic activities, and ultimately abandon Colin Clark's old paradigm based on the primary/secondary/tertiary sectors' distinction. Such a distinction has become an epistemological obstacle to the understanding of our societies. (Castells 1996, pp. 205–6)

The second problem with the traditional taxonomy is that it makes no distinction between industries that produce traded goods or services and those that produce nontraded ones. That distinction is critical, because the primary focus of this study is upon metropolitan areas. The concept of traded and nontraded goods and services comes from the economic literature on international trade. It simply recognizes that some products can be exported and imported, such as soybeans and music videos, and that some normally cannot, such as haircuts and garbage collection. The concept is useful for the analysis of subnational or regional economies and urban or metropolitan economies (Henderson 1988; Drennan 1999; Drennan et al. forthcoming). One can imagine a nation without significant external trade, but not a city. Food, fuel, and raw materials are almost never produced inside urban areas as conventionally defined. In a rough manner, all the industries of a metropolitan area can be sorted into those two sets: traded and nontraded goods and services. The traded category includes industries in which the output can be exported to or imported from elsewhere, elsewhere being any place outside the metropolitan area. Such industries are thus subject to competition from nonlocal producers for export markets as well as for the local market. The economic growth or decline of a metropolitan area is determined by the success or failure of its traded goods and services industries.

They are the drivers of the metropolitan economy. The industries producing non-traded goods and services are along for the ride. They simply respond to the expansion or contraction of the traded goods and services industries. Given that my central purpose is the analysis of metropolitan economies in the context of changing national and international aggregate demand, my taxonomy focuses only upon traded goods and services industries.

There are two broad sectors of traded goods and services in my revised taxonomy of industries: the goods production and distribution sector, and the information sector. Each of those are further partitioned into three functional groups. In the goods production and distribution sector, the three groups are: primary production (agriculture, forestry, fishing, and mining), manufacturing, and distribution (most transportation services plus wholesale trade). In the information sector, the three groups are financial producer services, other producer services, and advanced consumer services, which were defined in Chapter 1. Also, as noted there, the exact composition of each of the six groups, that is, the two-digit Standard Industrial Classification code industries included, are listed in the Appendix.

At first thought, advanced consumer services would appear to be nontraded, or residential, services. All metropolitan areas have hospitals, physicians' offices (health services, SIC 80), a private college or two (education, SIC 82), as well as bowling alleys, motion picture theaters (amusements, SIC 79), and a museum or zoo (museums, SIC 84). Typical as they may be of the modern urban landscape—as much so as gasoline stations and grocery stores—they are nonetheless "traded services," or, in the old-fashioned terminology, "export or basic" economic activities. Whether an industry is classified as traded or nontraded is *not* determined by whether a particular activity in a particular place produces income from nonresident establishments or households. It is so classified if the type of activity *could* normally be the source of such external income. Forty years ago, the health services industry in most metropolitan areas was not a significant source of income from nonresidents, although the nature of the activity made it a possible source of such income in a way that retail food stores were not and are not. Now, private health insurance pays for a significant share of health services provided at hospitals, clinics, and physicians' offices. The public programs of Medicare, health insurance for the elderly, and Medicaid, health insurance for the impoverished, pay for an even larger share of health care costs in metropolitan areas than does private insurance.

Both the private and the public health insurance dollars that flow into metropolitan areas to pay for health services represent income from nonresident establishments (insurance firms, the federal and state governments). The amounts are not trivial, and they have been increasing in importance. For comparison, look at a traditional major source of federal dollars for states, defense contracts. The total awarded in 1997 was $107 billion, down from $124 billion in 1990. California pulled in $18.5 billion of the 1997 total, far more than any other state. Like defense contracts, Medicare and Medicaid expenditures are distributed to health care providers across the nation. Unlike defense contracts, the amounts have been growing. Medicare spending in 1998 (all federal) was $209 billion and Medicaid spending (half federal, half state) was another $165 billion. Together they were 3 to 4 times larger than defense contracts. California received $22.6 billion of that Medicare total and about $6 billion in federal Medicaid money. In addition, California institutions received $1.9 billion in medical research grants from the National Institutes of Health (NIH) and $0.5 billion in grants from the National Science Foundation (NSF). Historically, California has been the major beneficiary of defense contracts, which mainly flow to manufacturing firms. Now, the annual dollars flowing from the federal government to firms and nonprofit organizations in California's advanced consumer services sector (hospitals, medical practitioners, and universities) dwarfs the state's defense contract dollars: $31 billion versus $19 billion (U.S. Census Bureau 1999). Just as senators, congressmen, and governors have struggled to increase their area's share of defense dollars, they are now also attuned to increasing or maintaining their share of federal health care dollars and of research dollars.

Obviously my taxonomy excludes many industries that I designate as nontraded, such as construction, electric and gas utilities, local passenger transportation, all of retail trade, personal and social services, and all government. For metropolitan areas, such a designation is sometimes incorrect. In resort areas such as Las Vegas and Orlando, retail trade is a traded service, because so much of the sales revenue comes from nonresidents. Similarly, in state capitals and in Washington, D.C., government is the major traded or exported service. Nonetheless, for the great majority of metropolitan areas, those industries are normally nontraded or local.

Sectoral Shift

My purpose in this section is to establish the increase in size of the information sector in the United States economy during the latter half of the twentieth century. The task is not easier done than said. The ideal illustration of the rise of the information sector would be a comparison of real output (GDP in constant dollars) in the information sector with real output in the goods production and distribution sector and with total real GDP over the period from the end of the Second World War until the present. However, for such a long timespan, the data comparability problems are formidable. Not the least problem is separating price changes from output changes for the component industries of my two traded goods and services sectors. Indeed, the National Income and Product Accounts for the United States, which are available back to 1929, include price deflators by industry only as far back as 1977, and then users are warned not to add industries over time (see BEA 1998b). Consequently, my evidence is less than ideal but far more persuasive than "information age" hype.

In Table 2.1, I present three measures of absolute and relative size for the two traded goods and services sectors (goods production and distribution sector and information sector) and for the entire economy. Those measures are GDP in current dollars, employment, and compensation of employees in current dollars. The data are shown for three time periods: 1948–52, 1971–75, and 1993–97. Each time period is an average of the five years noted in order to minimize business cycle effects.

The trends of all three variables tell the same story, namely, that the information sector was a small part of the economy in the earliest period but has become roughly as large as the goods production and distribution sector in the most recent period. For example, in the 1948–52 period, the information sector accounted for 12% of GDP while the goods production and distribution sector accounted for 54%. In the latest period, 1993–97, their shares of GDP were almost equal at 31% (information) and 33% (goods production and distribution). That pattern is repeated for the employment measure, persons engaged in production, and for the earnings measure, compensation of employees. Despite the caveats noted above about the difficulty of comparisons over time, it is undeniable that the information sector has become *relatively* much larger than it was

Table 2.1. Output, Employment, and Earnings of Traded Goods and Services Sectors, 1948–1997

	1948–52	1971–75	1993–97
Total GDP (billions current $)	287.6	1,270.1	6,677.3
GDP by sector			
Goods production and distribution	155.6	540.2	2,205.8
Information	33.3	242.7	2,081.4
Percentage of total GDP			
Goods production and distribution	54.1	42.5	33.0
Information	11.6	19.1	31.2
Total employment (millions)	59.9	81.8	121.8
Employment by sector			
Goods production and distribution	29.1	30.0	32.9
Information	5.8	13.9	33.0
Percentage of total employment			
Goods production and distribution	48.6	36.7	27.0
Information	9.7	17.0	27.1
Total earnings (billions current $)	163.4	808.7	4,229.0
Earnings by sector			
Goods production and distribution	85.0	328.8	1,311.3
Information	14.9	131.7	1,250.4
Percentage of total earnings			
Goods production and distribution	52.0	40.7	31.0
Information	9.1	16.3	29.6

Source: BEA 1998b.

50 years ago, while the goods production and distribution sector has become *relatively* much smaller than it was 50 years ago. Of course both are absolutely bigger than they were in the past. With the imperfect data at hand, it is not possible to say which of the two sectors is now bigger. The goods production and distribution sector appears to be absolutely bigger, but it is a close call.

All three of the goods production and distribution groups (primary production, manufacturing, and distribution) have had declining shares of GDP, employment, and earnings over the past half-century in the United States. Whereas all three of the information sector groups (financial producer services, other producer services, and advanced consumer services) have had increasing shares of GDP, employment, and earnings. The most dramatic declines in shares are in the primary production group. The most dramatic gains in shares are in the other producer services group. (For an extended version of Table 2.1 see "Supplementary Tables" 2002, Table S1.)

Although the GDP data in current dollars are not appropriate for comparisons of levels over time, for reasons explained above, the employment data are appropriate for such comparisons. The employment data, from the BEA, is the series entitled "persons engaged in production." In that data series, all part-time jobs are converted into full-time equivalents and the self-employed are added to the full-time equivalents. Industries vary widely in their use of part-time labor and in their proportions of self-employed. The more conventional employment data series, published by the U.S. Bureau of Labor Statistics, is a count of jobs that makes no distinction between part-time and full-time jobs and excludes the self-employed. Therefore, the more widely used BLS employment data can distort comparisons across groups of industries.

There were fewer than 6 million jobs in the information sector in the 1948–52 period but 29 million in the goods production and distribution sector. In the most recent period they were equal, with 33 million jobs each. Of course, the much slower expansion in goods production and distribution jobs partly reflects the much faster expansion in productivity (output per person) in that sector, a fact widely noted (Jones 1984; Norton 1986; Drennan 1999). Extending the comparison to component groups of the two sectors, in the 1948–52 period, employment in just the primary production group (agriculture and mining), 7 million, exceeded employment in the entire information sector. By 1993–97, each group of the information sector had much higher employment than the primary production group, which had an absolute decline over that long period ("Supplementary Tables," 2002, Table S1). The decline in the primary production group did not begin 50 years ago, of course, but much earlier. Using employment data, Singlemann (1974) shows that in 1920 the primary production group represented 29% of all national employment. Back then, almost three out of ten in the work force were engaged in farming, fishing, forestry, or mining. As noted in Chapter 1, the evolutionary view of economic development posits that such a long-term decline is inevitable. The manufacturing group continues to be the largest of the six groups, although it had an absolute decline of one-half million from the middle period, 1971–75, to the latest period. In that middle period, manufacturing employment, at 19.0 million, exceeded employment in the entire information sector by about 40%. However, in the latest period information sector employment exceeds manufacturing by about 70%. Those huge shifts in the composition of national employment have strongly contributed to the transformation of metropolitan areas, as I argue in a later chapter.

The post–World War II rise of the information sector compared with the

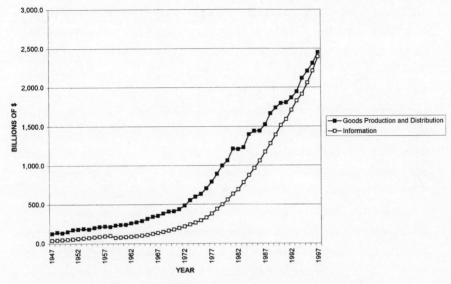

Figure 2.1 Annual GDP of Traded Goods and Services, by Sector, 1947–1997

goods production and distribution sector is dramatically illustrated in Figure 2.1. Rather than five-year averages for three points in time, Figure 2.1 shows the annual GDP in each of those two sectors over the 49 years from 1948 to 1997. Note that in the mid-1970s, the information sector was about one-half the size of the goods production and distribution sector, but by 1997 the two were about equal in size. The goods production and distribution sector exhibits cyclical sensitivity, with declines in recession years, whereas the information sector never shows a decline.

An important question that remains is whether *real* output of the manufacturing group as a share of real GDP has declined. It is important because the combination of stronger productivity growth with lower inflation in manufacturing could account for much of the relative decline in manufacturing current dollar GDP and employment (see "Supplementary Tables" 2002, Table S1). It is also important because much of the deindustrialization debate of the 1980s and its echoes are tied to the issue of whether manufacturing is diminishing as a share of real GDP. In the most careful critique of the deindustrialization hypothesis, Norton (1986) shows that manufacturing job loss in the 1970s and early 1980s was limited to the traditional manufacturing belt. Gains in the South and West kept the national total of manufacturing jobs flat. More to the point of this analysis, he also shows that in real dollars, "U.S. manufacturing output was about the same share of GNP in 1979, before the dollar appreciated, as in 1969 or 1959" (p. 12). His basis for that statement is the data series "constant dollar gross product originating by sector." However, the Bureau of Economic Analysis now publishes the constant dollar version of that data only back to 1977, as noted above, and it has been revised a few times since Norton wrote. Limiting the analysis to that period, and using five-year averages to smooth over business-cycle effects, the answer is that at least since the late 1970s, the real output in manufacturing as a percentage of real GDP has been declining. When Norton wrote (1986), the dollar had been rising strongly and U.S. manufacturing was suffering from that rise. The dollar came back down in the late 1980s and has been more or less stable in the 1990s. But manufacturing real output has not recovered its former relative share of real GDP. The stability of its share noted by Norton, from 1959 to 1979, is not evident in the revised data from 1977 to 1998, although the decline in share is glacierlike, dropping only 1.5 percentage points, from 18.4% in the 1977–81 period to 16.9% in the 1994–98 period (BEA 1997, 2000c).

Interactions among the Sectors

The sectoral shift highlighted above, which can be characterized as the transformation of the economy, is better understood by knowing how the traded goods and services groups of industries interact and how that interaction has changed over time. The national input-output tables compiled by the BEA provide a picture of that interaction at a few points in time. In the transactions matrix of a national input-output table, every cell shows a dollar entry, which is annual sales of output of the industry named in the row to the industry named in the column or to a final demand sector (consumption, government purchases, investment expenditures, and exports). So any row shows the dollar distribution of the output of the industry named in that row among the industries and final demand sectors that purchased its output. The published input-output tables for the United States are produced every five years with quite a lag. The most recent tables, published in 2000, present data for the year 1996.

I have taken the U.S. input-output tables for 1972 and 1996, which split the economy into 85 detailed industries, and have aggregated the transactions ma-

Table 2.2. Input-Output Percentages for 1972 and 1996

| | Input Sector | | | |
| | 1972 | | 1996 | |
Output Sector	Goods Production and Distribution	Information	Goods Production and Distribution	Information
Goods Production and Distribution				
Primary production	82.5	1.4	79.6	2.0
Manufacturing	40.9	2.1	41.1	6.1
Distribution	34.3	2.1	37.9	5.9
Information				
Financial producer services	14.9	17.9	10.6	29.2
Other producer services	44.0	22.9	18.7	33.6
Advanced consumer services	1.1	6.9	1.4	7.1

Source: BEA 1979, 2000a.

trices into the six broad groups of traded goods and services industries and one residual group. A summary comparing the two years is shown in Table 2.2. Over those 24 years, the three information sector groups had much larger increases in production for intermediate use and in value added than did the three goods production and distribution groups. That was also true for growth in final demand, except that financial producer services growth was not far above manufacturing growth. That corresponds with the trends observed in GDP, employment, and earnings reported above. (For more detail about both years, see "Supplementary Tables" 2002, Table S2.)

For each of the six groups, the table shows the percentage of output of that group that was sold to each of the two sectors—goods production and distribution, and information—in 1972 and 1996. The percentages do not sum to 100, because some output of each group was sold to sectors not shown, namely non-traded goods and services and final demand. Each percentage entry indicates the relative importance of each sector as a customer for the output of a group. In 1972, the information sector was of trivial importance as a customer for the output of every group in the goods production and distribution sector: primary production, manufacturing, and distribution. Only 2% or less of output in each of those gorups was sold to the information sector. By 1996, although still small, the shares of output from those same three groups sold to the information sector had all risen. For manufacturing and distribution, the output sold to the information sector rose from 2% to 6%; the rise was less for primary production.

Thus, the information sector has become a relatively more important customer for the output of the three groups in the goods production and distribution sector than it had been in 1972.

The opposite has happened with the three groups of the information sector. In 1972, the goods production and distribution sector was of mixed importance as a customer for the output of the three information sector groups. Financial producer services sold 15% of its output to the goods production and distribution sector; other producer services sold almost one-half, 44%, of its output to the goods production and distribution sector, while the advanced consumer services group sold only 1% of its output to the goods production and distribution sector. By 1996, however, there was a marked drop in the share of output sold to the goods production and distribution sector by the financial producer services group: from 15% to 11%. The drop is more dramatic for the other producer services group: from 44% of its output sold to the goods production and distribution sector in 1972 to 19% in 1996. There was hardly any change for the advanced consumer services group. Thus, the goods production and distribution sector has become a relatively less important customer for the output of two of the three groups in the information sector. For the third group, advanced consumer services, the good production and distribution sector was of trivial importance as a customer in both years.

One implication of these findings is that the strong growth in producer services, financial and other, is *not* accounted for by the vertical disintegration of manufacturing whereby producer services formerly produced in-house become contracted out to producer services firms. That hypothesis has been proposed by Scott (1998). If it were correct, I would expect to see a substantial rise in the relative share of producer service output sold to manufacturing from 1972 to 1996. Instead, the detailed input-output tables show the same pattern as my summary, Table 2.2, namely a drop in the shares of producer services output sold to manufacturing. For other producer services, the drop is from 24% to 10%, and for financial producer services, from 5% to 4%. Like Scott, Sassen (1991) argues that vertical disintegration and outsourcing in manufacturing have expanded demand for financial and other producer services. In an otherwise excellent book, *The New Dollars and Dreams* (1998), Frank Levy infers that growth in business services (part of the other producer services group) reflects a substitution of service firm output for what was formerly manufacturing output. "The growth of business service employment underlines the ambiguous meaning of some of these shifts. If the kitchen stove company had an accountant on its payroll, she would have been tabulated as a manufacturing employee. If the accountant had left to join an accounting firm, taking the stove company's business with her, she would be retabulated as a service sector employee even though she did the same job" (p. 69). This reflects the same view as Scott (1998) and Sassen (1991), namely that growth in producer services was a consequence of manufacturing firms' outsourcing work formerly done in-house. The input-output data do not support their claim.

The absolute importance, in dollars of purchased output, and how that has changed over time is also of interest. In 1972 the manufacturing group sold $16 billion of its output to the information sector, while the information sector sold $39 billion of its output to the manufacturing group. Thus, in dollars, manufacturing was a more important customer for the information sector than vice versa. But by 1996, the manufacturing group's sales to the information sector, $222 billion, were slightly higher than the information sector's sales to manufacturing, $215 billion. So, as a *customer* for manufacturing output, the information sector has become somewhat more important in dollar terms than is the manufacturing group as a *customer* for information sector output (BEA 1979, 2000a).

Given that the information sector has become as important a customer, an upstream buyer, of manufacturing output as it is a supplier of inputs for manufacturing in dollar terms, the rapid rise of output in the information sector has contributed to output growth in manufacturing. As Jones (1984) pointed out, much of the growth in manufacturing output has been driven by demand for capital goods in the information sector, such as computers and surgical instruments, as well as for intermediate goods, such as floppy disks and disposable syringes. "Without the huge expansion in services and the commensurate rise in demand for capital and intermediate goods in services, the growth in manufacturing would have been much less than it was" (Jones 1984, p. 9). The irony here is that Scott (1998), Sassen (1991), and Levy (1998) have argued that increased information sector output is a substitute for manufacturing output, as producer service functions formerly performed within manufacturing firms are contracted to outside suppliers (outsourcing). But the input-output data do not support that view. Rather, they support the view that the two are complements, not substi-

Table 2.3. Impact Analysis of 1996 Input-Output Tables
(billions $)

Group	PRM	MFG	DIST	PSFIN	PSOTH	ACS	Other	Total
Primary production (PRM)	26.20	6.62	2.54	3.56	1.70	0.24	2.17	43.03
Manufacturing (MFG)	3.16	33.34	3.58	1.58	2.28	0.18	2.02	46.14
Distribution (DIST)	0.45	3.70	22.74	1.67	3.08	0.17	1.65	33.46
Financial producer services (PSFIN)	0.28	1.43	0.58	24.90	2.79	0.13	1.87	31.98
Other producer services (PSOTH)	0.34	2.99	0.90	1.74	24.41	0.57	1.31	32.26
Advanced consumer services (ACS)	0.52	4.00	1.19	2.76	3.21	20.96	1.90	34.54
All other	0.99	4.40	1.23	1.48	1.84	0.11	21.79	31.84

Source: Computed using Leontief inverse matrix derived from "Supplementary Tables" 2002, Table 52, based on BEA 2000a.
Note: The effect of an increase of $20 billion in final demand for group named in row upon output of each group named in column.

tutes. Other studies support that claim. In their recent article on the shift to a service economy, Garcia-Mila and McGuire (1998) note that "relative employment in producer services within manufacturing has increased in recent years. From the available evidence, it appears that manufacturing is increasingly dependent on services; manufacturers are producing more services internally and are also purchasing more services in the market" (p. 355).

Aggregating input-output transactions tables for 1996, I have computed the matrix of direct and indirect input coefficients, or the Leontief inverse matrix, for that year. The Leontief inverse is used to measure the effect of a given change in final demand in any sector upon total output in each sector. Using the Leontief inverse for 1996, I have simulated the effects upon total output of an increase in final demand of $20 billion in each of the six traded goods and services groups (Table 2.3). The $20 billion rise is assumed to occur in only one group at a time. The largest effects on total output occur with the final demand increase (always $20 billion) in the primary production group and the manufacturing group. The exogenous rise of final demand in the primary production group increases total output by $43 billion, and the rise of final demand in manufacturing increases total output by $46 billion. For each of the remaining four groups and for the residual group, the effects upon total output of a $20 billion increase in final demand are much smaller, ranging from $32 to $35 billion. The old-fashioned Keynesian interpretation of that simulation would be that boosting final demand in the primary production or the manufacturing group provides a bigger "multiplier" effect upon total output than the same size stimulus for any other group. But that naïvely assumes excess capacity and no price response in any group.

More interesting than the "bang for the buck" analysis is the low level of interaction among most groups. The primary production and the manufacturing groups do appear to react to increases in final demand in one another. For example, the $20 billion rise in primary production final demand raises manufacturing output $6.6 billion. No other group (besides itself) has such a large impact on manufacturing output. The closest is the residual group, where a $20 billion rise in final demand boosts manufacturing output $4.4 billion. The three groups of the information sector have little effect upon one another or upon the groups of the goods production and distribution sector, with one exception. A rise in final demand for advanced consumer services increases manufacturing output by $4.0 billion. The absence of strong effects in other groups from a final demand change, with the exceptions noted, suggests a low level of inter-industry transactions across groups. That may be the case. But it is perhaps as likely that the absence of strong effects across most groups that do not produce goods reflects a problem with the data. The U.S. input-output tables provide very detailed industry breakdowns in the primary production and manufacturing groups but far too little detail in the other groups.

When input-output accounting and analysis was first developed by Wasilly Leontief in 1941 (for which he was awarded the Nobel Memorial Prize), the goods production and distribution sector dwarfed the information sector. Nonetheless, according to the Oxford *Dictionary of Economics* (Black 1997), input-output is defined as the "study of the flows of goods and *services* (my emphasis) between different sectors of the economy" (p. 238). In the most recent input-output summary tables published by the BEA (2000a), the economy is partitioned into 96 industries. What I have defined as the goods production and distribution sector accounts for 66 of those 96 industries, while what I have defined as the information sector accounts for only 12 of the 96. The remaining 18 fall into the nontraded goods and services category. Given the current size of the information sector, that is, about as large as the goods production and distribution sector, that treatment in the input-output accounts is not balanced. Indeed, 52 of the 66 goods production and distribution industries are manufacturing industries.

Large Firms in the Two Sectors

Each year *Fortune* publishes a list of the 1,000 largest corporations in the United States, ranked by revenues. The 1,000 are also sorted by industry. I have grouped those firms into the information sector and the goods production and distribution sector and further into the six groups of industries (see Table 2.4). Not all 1,000 corporations are included in my grouping, because some are classified in nontraded industries, such as construction, electric and gas utilities, and retail trade. Half of the largest 1,000 corporations are classified in the goods production and distribution sector, one-quarter in the information sector, and the remaining one-quarter are not in either sector. Revenues in 2001 for the 481 large goods production and distribution firms were $4,082 billion, and about one-half that amount for the 255 large information sector firms. Employment by the

Table 2.4. *Fortune* 1,000 Firms' Revenues and Employment,
by Traded Goods and Services Group, 2000

Sector and Group	Number of Firms	Revenues (billions $)	Employment (thousands)
Goods production and distribution			
Primary production	46	260	870
Manufacturing	349	3,051	10,418
Distribution	86	771	2,144
TOTAL	481	4,082	13,432
Information			
Financial producer services	145	1,549	3,130
Other producer services	68	522	2,032
Advanced consumer services	42	269	1,345
TOTAL	255	2,350	6,507

Source: Fortune 2001.

goods production and distribution firms was over 13 million, and again the large information sector firms had about one-half as much employment. Interestingly, the average firm is larger in the information sector in revenue terms.

Manufacturing accounts for 349 of the 1,000 largest corporations. No other industry group is as large. But another perspective on that fact is that in 2000 *only* one-third of the 1,000 largest U.S. corporations were manufacturers. Because the *Fortune* list of 1,000 began only a few years ago, comparisons with two or three decades past are not easily made. But even in the first year, 1994, the list had a much larger number of manufacturing corporations than in 2000: 423 compared with 349. In view of the other evidence of the rise of the information sector and the relative decline of manufacturing, it is doubtless true that thirty years ago the list of 1,000 largest corporations would have included even many more manufacturing firms than in 1994.

The *Fortune* 1,000 list is limited to publicly held corporations, and so it understates the importance of the information sector in the economy. For example, the list excludes accounting firms and management consulting firms, both of which are part of the other producer services group of the information sector and both of which include some very large firms. The "Big 5" accounting firms together had 1999 revenues of $22 billion. The largest management consulting firm, Andersen Consulting, had revenues of $6.1 billion that year. That would place it in about the top one-third of the *Fortune* 1,000 ranking. The list also excludes nonprofit organizations, such as hospitals and universities, some of which have annual revenues above many *Fortune* 1,000 firms and all of which are part of the information sector.

International Dimensions of the Information Sector

Given that the information sector has become as large as the goods production and distribution sector in the United States at the end of the twentieth century, one would expect that it has become more important in measures of international economic activity for the United States. The data on foreign trade, on U.S. multinational corporations, and on foreign direct investment in the United States do in fact support that expectation. Similarly, large organizations of the information sector have become comparable in size with large industrial corporations, and many have strong international operations. I use the more inclusive term *organization* rather than *firm* because the advanced consumer services part of the information sector has large health institutions, universities, and museums that are nonprofit organizations.

Michael Porter (*The Competitive Advantage of Nations* 1990) has argued that international success in services is as valuable to a nation's competitive advantage as international success in manufacturing. He points out that service industries engaged in international trade employ highly skilled labor in their home country. That is certainly the case for the United States, for which the export of services has been growing faster than the export of goods over the past two decades. That is particularly true of information services and royalties and license fees. Information service exports include financial services, insurance, telecommunication services, and business and professional services. In other words, all of the industries included in my financial producer services and other producer services groups. The two major industries of the advanced consumer services group, health and education, are also included in information service exports. What I call information service exports are labeled "other private service exports" in the United States trade statistics, to distinguish them from the service exports of travel expenditures, passenger fares, other transportation, and royalties and license fees (BEA 2001b). Royalties and license fees, including those for industrial processes, are obviously information exports, and so I add them to the information service exports to get a measure of total information exports.

Exports of goods from the United States expanded 8% per year from 1978

Table 2.5. U.S. International Trade in Goods and Information Services, 1978 and 2000

(billions $)

	1978	2000	Average Annual Change (%)
Exports			
Agriculture	29.9	52.8	2.6
High-tech	18.2	217.6	11.9
Other goods	94.0	501.8	7.9
Total goods exports	142.1	772.2	8.0
Information services	4.7	107.6	15.3
Royalties and license fees	5.9	38.0	8.8
Total information exports	10.6	145.6	12.7
Imports			
Agriculture	12.1	32.8	4.6
High-tech	7.2	217.6	16.8
Other goods	156.7	974.0	8.7
Total goods imports	176.0	1,224.4	9.2
Information services	2.6	54.9	14.9
Royalties and license fees	0.7	16.1	15.3
Total information imports	3.2	71.0	15.1
Trade balance (+/−)			
Agriculture	+17.8	+20.0	
High-tech	+11.0	—	
Other goods	−62.7	−472.2	
Total goods balance	−33.9	−452.2	
Information services	+2.1	+52.7	
Royalties and license fees	+5.2	+21.9	
Total information balance	+7.4	+74.6	

Source: BEA 2001b.

through 2000 (see Table 2.5). Of that total, agricultural exports had the slowest growth, under 3% per year and high-tech exports the fastest growth per year, 12%. What I label high-tech exports includes computers, semiconductors, telecommunications equipment, office and business machines, scientific and medical equipment, and civilian aircraft, engines, and parts. Over that same twenty-two years, information exports grew faster: 13% per year. Of the two components, exports of information services increased 15% per year and royalties and license fees increased 9%. The relative growth of goods and information exports is highlighted in Figure 2.2, showing that information exports are almost 90% higher than they were in 1992 while goods exports are 50% higher. Although growing faster, the information exports are not nearly so large as the goods exports. Goods exports were $772 billion in 2000, and information exports $146 billion.

The shifting mix in the foreign trade of the United States reflects the shifting mix of traded goods and services in the nation's output. Back in 1978, the agricultural part of goods exports was six times larger than the export of information services: $30 billion compared with $5 billion. Although both are larger now, information service exports in 2000 were twice as big as agricultural exports. Total information exports of $146 billion do not match the high-tech exports of $218 billion. But on a trade balance basis, information services carry more weight. The U.S. trade balance (exports minus imports) on all goods was −$452 billion in 2000. The last positive trade balance on goods was in 1975 (BEA 1999b). Within the goods category, the high-tech trade balance was zero, exports being equal to imports. The agriculture trade balance was a positive $20 billion. The contribution of the information sector towards offsetting the large negative balance on goods was +$75 billion (see Table 2.5).

Some large components of the information sector's exports for two years, 1986 and 2000, are presented in Table 2.6. The largest component—business, professional, and technical services—covers exports by the industries included in the other producer services group. Growth in those exports averaged 16% annually, 1986 to 2000. The second largest component is financial services exports: $17 billion in 2000. It has expanded faster than 12% per year since 1986. Large

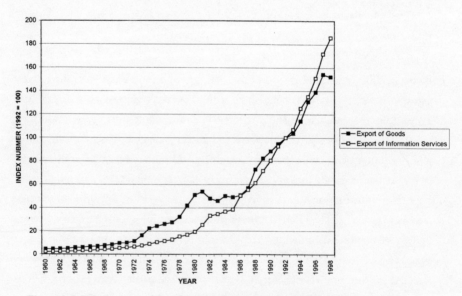

Figure 2.2 U.S. Exports of Goods and Information, 1960–1998

Table 2.6. Information Sector Exports by Type, 1986 and 2000
(billions $)

	1986	1998	Average Annual Change (%)
Information service exports			
Business, professional, and technical services	3.7	28.0	15.6
Financial services	3.3	17.0	12.4
Education	3.5	10.3	8.0
Telecommunication	1.8	3.8	5.5
Insurance, net (premiums less losses)	1.4	2.4	3.9
Royalties and license fees for exports			
Other royalties and license fees (copyrights, trademarks, franchises, other intangible property rights)	0.7[a]	7.0	17.9
Industrial process royalties and license fees	1.6[a]	4.4	7.5

Source: BEA 2001b.
[a]1987.

as those financial service exports are, they do not include interest income paid by foreign banks to U.S. residents. Education is the third largest component of information services exports, totaling $10 billion in 2000. That represents tuition and fees of foreign students enrolled in U.S. educational institutions, both public and private. Almost all of those export earnings are from institutions of higher education. Growth has been 8% annually since 1986, despite the strong dollar and rising tuition and fees at American universities. Just as the high-tech exports are not ubiquitous, neither are the education exports. That is, some urban places, such as Boston, are major sources of education service exports because of their high concentration of major universities that attract students from around the world. Some urban places, such as Youngstown, lack major universities and so are not sources of education service exports.

There is only one component of the advanced consumer services group shown in the detailed export data: education. However, the royalties and license fees exports shown, separate from industrial process royalties and fees, include intellectual property income from motion pictures, music, and entertainment events, all part of the advanced consumer services group. That part has been expanding 18% annually since 1986.

Another aspect of globalization is the increased international reach of U.S. corporations. The gross product of multinational corporations (MNCs) is grow-

Table 2.7. U.S.-Based Multinational Corporations (MNCs)
and Their Majority-Owned Foreign Affiliates (MOFAs)
(billions $)

	1989	1998	Change (%)
Gross product of MNCs			
Goods production and distribution	988	1,354	37.0
Information	130	250	92.0
All industries	1,365	2,119	55.0
Gross product of MOFAs			
Goods production and distribution	286	400	39.9
Information	22	64	190.0
All industries	320	511	59.7

Source: BEA 2000d.

Table 2.8. Foreign Direct Investment in the United States, by Traded Goods
and Services Group, 1997 and 2000
(billions $)

Sector and Group	1997	2000	Change (%)
Goods production and distribution			
Primary production	55.3	105.9	91.5
Manufacturing	270.1	496.6	83.9
Distribution	95.3	122.8	28.9
TOTAL	420.7	725.3	72.4
Information			
Financial producer services	191.4	305.4	59.6
Other producer services	24.1	109.8	355.6
Advanced consumer services	7.9	11.1	40.5
TOTAL	223.4	426.3	90.8
Total all industries	681.8	1,238.6	81.7

Source: BEA 2001c.

ing very rapidly. I have sorted the MNC industry data on gross product into the two sectors: goods production and distribution, and information (see Table 2.7). MNCs in the goods production and distribution sector account for a far larger share of MNC gross product (64%) than do the MNCs in the information sector. However, gross product of MNCs in the information sector has been growing twice as fast as the former's since 1989. The same pattern holds true for the majority-owned foreign affiliates (MOFAs) of U.S. multinationals.

Foreign direct investment (FDI) in the United States by foreign corporations or individuals is yet another aspect of globalization. As is true of trade and U.S. multinationals, broad measures of FDI exhibit growth well above growth of the entire economy. I have sorted the FDI data into the two sectors (goods produc-

Table 2.9. World's Ten Largest Banks, Advertising Holding Companies,
and Manangement Consulting Firms, 1999

Bank	Nation	Assets (billions $)
Deutsche Bank	Germany	732.5
UBS	Switzerland	685.9
Citigroup	United States	668.6
Bank of America	United States	617.7
Bank of Tokyo-Mitsubishi	Japan	579.8
ABN Amro Holding	Netherlands	504.1
HSBC Holdings	United Kingdom	483.1
Fuji Bank	Japan	481.4
Credit Suisse Group	Switzerland	474.0
Intl Nederlanden Groep	Netherlands	460.8

Advertising Holding Companies	Nation	Gross Income (billions $)
Omnicom Group	United States	5.7
Interpublic Group of Companies	United States	5.1
WPP Group PLC	United Kingdom	4.8
Havas Advertising	France	2.4
Dentsu	Japan	2.1
Young and Rubicam	United States	1.9
B Com 3 Group	United States	1.9
Grey Advertising	United States	1.6
True North	United States	1.5
Publicis Communications	France	1.4

Management Consulting Firms	Nation	Revenues (billions $)
Andersen Consulting	United States	6.6
Ernst and Young	United States	5.5
Deloitte Consulting	United States	3.6
McKinsey and Company	United States	2.2
PricewaterhouseCoopers	United States	2.1
KPMG	United States	1.7
Booz Allan Hamilton	United States	1.3
CSC	United States	NA
Cap Gemini	France	NA
A.T. Kearney	United States	NA

Source: Institutional Investor International 1999; *Advertising Age* 2000; Dun and Bradstreet 1999; *Ward's Business Directory* 1999.

tion and distribution, and information) and then into the six groups of industries. For the goods production and distribution sector, foreign direct investment in the United States expanded 72% in the three years from 1997 to 2000 (see Table 2.8). During the same period, that measure for the information sector expanded 91%. Although the information sector's part of FDI is growing faster, it is still smaller than the goods production and distribution sector's part: $426 billion versus $725 billion in 2000.

A number of industries within the information sector are dominated by large firms for which the world, rather than just the United States, is their market. Commercial banking, advertising, and management consulting are such industries (see Table 2.9). Among the ten largest banks in the world in 1999, the third and fourth largest were U.S. banks (Citigroup and Bank of America). With the recent merger of Chase with J. P. Morgan, a third U.S. bank ranks in the top ten. The large U.S. firms do not dominate world banking as they dominate advertising and management consulting. Six of the top ten advertising holding companies in the world are U.S. firms. The first- and second-ranked firms, Omnicom Group and Interpublic Group, are U.S. firms, with 1999 revenues of $5.7 and $5.1 billion respectively. Only one of the world's largest management consulting firms is not a U.S. firm: Cap Gemini of France. Revenues of the largest U.S consulting firms range from $6.6 billion for first-ranked Andersen Consulting to $1.3 billion for seventh-ranked Booz Allan Hamilton.

The Information Sector after the Stock Market Decline

In March 2000, the NASDAQ stock market index dropped sharply and has not recovered. On September 5th, 2001, the week before the destruction of the World Trade Center towers by suicidal terrorists sent shock waves through financial markets, it was 65% below its high in March 2000. Many of the "new economy" high-tech stocks are listed on the NASDAQ National Market rather than the New York Stock Exchange, most notably Microsoft. The decline in stock prices has not been limited to NASDAQ shares, although they have been hit the hardest. A broad-based measure, the Standard and Poors Index of 500 Stocks, was above 1,500 in March 2000. On September 5th it was 1,132, a 26% drop from its high. Most of the damage has been visited upon the high-tech stocks, that is, those related to computers, telecommunication equipment, computer software, and e-commerce, all the darlings of investors in the late 1990s. Many high-flying "dot-com" start-ups that were bid upward in price immediately upon their market debuts in the late 1990s have since fallen by almost 100%, that is, to zero. NASDAQ has delisted a number of stocks since March of 2000. A stock is delisted when its price very closely approaches zero.

A few anecdotes capture the general debacle. Webvan, an on-line supermarket with home delivery, was first listed on NASDAQ in June 1999. One year later it acquired a competing online supermarket for $1 billion. Over the next year Webvan's share price plummeted 99% to less than $0.25 per share, wiping out $3.5 billion in shareholder wealth. In order to keep the share price above one dollar, the minimum price to retain a listing on NASDAQ, the Webvan management did a reverse stock split of one for 25. That means stockholders received one new share for every 25 old shares. It did not help. Webvan shut down in July 2001, laying off its 2,000 employees. In its short life, Webvan used up $1.2 billion in real money.

The decline was not limited to new Internet firms with no real assets. Corning, the venerable glass manufacturer located in upstate New York, was founded after the Civil War. In the 1990s, Corning's output of fiber-optic cable and the telecommunication equipment that goes with fiber overshadowed all of its other glass-related products. When the bubble burst, Corning was hit hard, like Lucent and Nortel, other major producers of fiber-optic cable and related telecommunication equipment. In July 2001, Corning announced a whopping $5.1 billion charge and declared no dividend for the first time since the company went public in 1945. Corning also laid off 1,000 workers at its home site, one-eighth of its work force there, and more around the country. Its share price has dropped from $113 in September 2000 to $15 in July 2001.

The blunt question for this study is: Does the stock market drop indicate that the information sector, as described in this book, will grow more slowly than the goods production and distribution sector over the coming decades? In other words, will the trend of the past half-century of information sector growth greater than goods production and distribution growth be reversed? That is not likely unless world trade and labor productivity slide into a relentless long decline, putting more labor back into factories, mines, and farms to get the same or less output.

The stock market decline was not a direct hit on the information sector as defined here, although it was a direct hit on what has come to be called the high-tech sector. Two industries in the high-tech sector, computer hardware and telecommunication equipment, are in the manufacturing group. High-tech also includes computer software, research, and biotechnology firms, all of which are classified here in the other producer services group. Thus, the stock market decline was most severe in two of my six traded goods and services groups: manufacturing and other producer services. Neither all manufacturing firms nor all

Table 2.10. Market Value of Publicly Listed Stocks on New York Stock Exchange
and NASDAQ, by Group, February and March 2000 and April 2001
(billions $)

New York Stock Exchange	March 2000	April 2001	Change (%)
Goods production and distribution			
Primary production	199.4	287.3	44.1
Manufacturing	5,534.7	5,474.4	−1.1
Distribution	190.6	205.4	7.8
TOTAL	5,924.7	5,967.1	0.7
Information			
Financial producer services	2,296.8	2,630.1	14.5
Other producer services	1,518.6	1,196.5	−21.2
Advanced consumer services	169.7	203.6	20.0
TOTAL	3,985.1	4,030.2	1.1
NASDAQ	February 2000	April 2001	Change (%)
Goods production and distribution			
Primary production	12.6	16.7	32.5
Manufacturing	2,928.6	1,432.1	−51.1
Distribution	60.0	53.1	11.5
TOTAL	3,001.2	1,501.9	−50.0
Information			
Financial producer services	226.6	261.5	15.4
Other producer services	1,762.8	1,170.7	−33.6
Advanced consumer services	34.8	38.6	10.9
TOTAL	2,024.2	1,470.8	−27.3

Source: Unpublished data provided by New York Stock Exchange, Research Department, New York, and NASDAQ Stock Market, Gaithersburg, MD.

other producer service firms are high-tech. But on the NASDAQ National Market, there is a high concentration of high-tech manufacturing firms and high-tech other producer service firms. So it is on the NASDAQ National Market that the manufacturing group and the other producer service group show severe declines. On the larger market, the New York Stock Exchange, those two groups also declined, but much less so. The market value of shares outstanding, sorted into each of the six traded goods and services groups, on the New York Stock Exchange and on the NASDAQ National Market are presented in Table 2.10. The aggregate market values at the peak (March 2000 for the New York Stock Exchange, February 2000, for NASDAQ) and the most recent period for which I have data (April 2001) are shown. Not all listed shares are included, because many of them are classified in nontraded goods and services industries such as retail trade and public utilities.

The only group for which the NASDAQ market value exceeded the New York

Stock Exchange market value at the peak was the other producer services group. That is no longer the case. The NASDAQ firms in the other producer services group lost one-third of their value, $600 billion. That group also had the biggest loss on the New York Stock Exchange, −21%. The NASDAQ firms in the manufacturing group, heavily weighted with high-tech firms, fared even worse, losing one-half their value, $1.5 trillion. The New York Stock Exchange firms in the manufacturing group, a far more diverse set, lost only 1%.

Unlike the other producer services group, the financial producer services group was unscathed by the market decline on both the NASDAQ and the New York Stock Exchange, rising about 15%. Note that the financial group is far larger than the other producer service group on the New York Stock Exchange, while the opposite is the case on the NASDAQ. That reflects the preponderance of high-tech firms listed on the NASDAQ.

The primary production group, although tiny in both markets, showed large gains, while the other groups had either respectable or catastrophic performances. The rise in energy prices has boosted the value of energy stocks, which are classified in the primary production group. The smallest market value on both stock markets shown is for firms in the advanced consumer services group. That is because the biggest parts of advanced consumer services are private health services and private education, industries in which the large institutions are nonprofit hospitals and universities. As such, they are not publicly traded and do not issue ownership shares. The publicly listed firms in the advanced consumer services group tend to be in the entertainment industry, such as Walt Disney, or in for-profit health services. Many of the dot-com firms irrationally favored by investors before the stock market drop, such as Amazon.com, are not represented in Table 2.10, because they are classified in retail trade, a nontraded category. Some are reported to have lost 80% of their value, some are in bankruptcy, and some have vanished.

The point of this exercise is to show that the "new economy" touted by stock market gurus, as well as by Alan Greenspan (Krugman 2001), and the information sector analyzed in this book are not the same thing, although they do intersect. Consequently, the stock market drop concentrated as it was in high-tech firms, hit only one group of the information sector: other producer services. The biggest drop was suffered by high-tech manufacturing firms, which are part of the goods production and distribution sector. And perhaps the biggest drop of all was among the retail dot-com firms, which are neither in the information sector nor the goods production and distribution sector.

Two economists with the Council of Economic Advisors have argued that the high-tech stock market drop does not signify that the expanded use of information technology (IT) has failed or is in retreat.

> The collapse of many Internet companies has caused some to argue that the new e-conomy has disappeared, but this is a misreading of what has happened. . . . Is there a new e-conomy? Statements such as "The business cycle is dead," "All the old skills are obsolete," "Only new companies can survive," and "The rules of economics have all changed" are all false, and any "new e-conomy" based on assuming they are true does not exist. However, there has been a wave of innovation, much of it tied to IT, driving greatly improved economic performance in the recent expansion, affecting old and new firms. This statement is correct, and in that sense there is a new e-conomy. (Baily and Lawrence 2001, p. 311)

3 | The Information Sector in Metropolitan Economies

In Chapter 2 I showed that the information sector of the U.S. economy has increased in absolute and relative size over the past few decades, and that it is now about as large as the goods production and distribution sector. I described the international dimensions of the U.S. information sector, showing its increasing importance in foreign trade, foreign direct investment, and lastly the expanded foreign reach of large U.S. firms in the information sector. In this chapter and the next three chapters, I move from a national perspective to a metropolitan perspective. The central point is that the evolution of the national economy has profoundly affected the economic fortunes of metropolitan economies, as one might expect, given that more than three-quarters of the nation's population is in metropolitan territory.

Table 2.1 documented the national expansion of the information sector compared with the goods production and distribution sector over the second half of the twentieth century. The metropolitan dimension of that shift in the composition of traded goods and services is captured for a shorter period (due to data limitations) in Table 3.1. Earnings in each of the six groups that compose the information sector and the goods production and distribution sector are shown for the sum of all metropolitan areas in 1969 and 1996. The earnings are in 1992 dollars. Just as the national data showed, the goods production and distribution sector has become relatively smaller in metropolitan areas while the information sector has become relatively larger. In 1969, the goods production and distribution sector was more than twice as big as the information sector, accounting for 42% of metropolitan earnings compared with 19% for the information sector.

Table 3.1. Earnings by Traded Goods and Services Groups
for All Metropolitan Areas, for 1969 and 1996
(billions 1992 $)

	1969		1996	
Sector and Group	Amount	Percentage of Total	Amount	Percentage of Total
Goods production and distribution				
Primary	47	2.3	60	1.7
Manufacturing	574	28.6	611	17.3
Distribution	216	10.8	357	10.1
TOTAL	837	41.7	1,028	29.1
Information				
Financial producer services	118	5.9	317	9.0
Other producer services	131	6.5	521	14.8
Advanced consumer services	124	6.2	406	11.5
TOTAL	373	18.6	1,244	35.2
All traded goods and services earnings	1,210	60.3	2,272	64.3
Nontraded earnings	795	39.7	1,260	35.7
TOTAL EARNINGS	2,005	100.0	3,532	100.0

Source: Computed from BEA 1998a.

By 1996, the goods production and distribution share of earnings was down to 29% while the information sector's share was up to 35%. Unlike the nation, where the shares of output, employment, and earnings had become roughly equal by the end period, for metropolitan areas the information sector had become decidedly larger by 1996. That reflects the fact that two of the goods production and distribution groups, manufacturing and especially primary production, are less concentrated in metropolitan territory than are the other groups. Note that, as with the nation, all groups show an absolute rise in real earnings. The manufacturing group continues to be the largest of the six, although its share of metropolitan earnings dropped from 29% in 1969 to 17% in 1996.

A central question for this study, addressed in this chapter and the next, is the extent to which metropolitan areas are specialized in any of the six traded goods and services groups. A second question is whether such specialization matters, that is, does specialization enhance the level and the growth of metropolitan per capita income or the growth of metropolitan population and employment?

Theories favoring specialization as an important source of productivity enhancement have a long history in economics (see Marshall 1890; Schumpeter 1942; Arrow 1962; Roemer 1986; and Porter 1990). The unifying idea among those writers is that technical knowledge is an external benefit or positive spillover among firms in the same industry. Marshall (1890) expressed the idea in a spatial context, succinctly restated by Glaeser et al.: "the concentration of an industry in a city helps knowledge spillovers between firms and, therefore, the growth of that industry and of that city" (Glaeser et al. 1992).

The theory that concentration of an industry in a city, specialization, enhances urban growth has been challenged by Chinitz (1961) and Jacobs (1969), among others (Rosenberg 1963; Scherer 1982; Bairoch 1988). They argue that diversity, not specialization, stimulates knowledge spillovers and thus enhances urban growth.

In the 1990s there have been several empirical studies of this issue. In a review article, Quigley (1998) cites some studies in which city diversity and city size favor growth. In perhaps the most thorough of those empirical studies, the effect of specialization upon metropolitan *growth* is explored by Glaeser et al. (1992). They concluded that diversity was better for metropolitan growth than specialization, thus supporting the views of Jacobs (1969) and Chinitz (1961). However, Henderson, Kuncoro, and Turner (1995) found a more mixed picture. For cities with concentrations of mature capital goods manufacturing industries, past concentration enhances employment growth while diversity does not. For high-tech manufacturing industries in cities, past diversity, not concentration enhances growth. In a very recent empirical investigation of that issue (Drennan et al. forthcoming), my co-authors and I concluded that some specializations do raise the level of metropolitan income, although the time period matters.

Although the empirical evidence tilts in favor of diversity for enhancing urban productivity and growth, the pro-diversity empirical studies cited focus almost exclusively on specialization in goods production (manufacturing industries) and goods distribution (wholesale trade industries). That is too narrow a perspective to support a generalization about specialization. That is particularly the case because of the long-term relative decline in goods production and goods distribution as urban specialties, as I have shown in Chapter 2 and elsewhere (Drennan 1999). Glaeser et al. (1992) recognize that the narrow scope of their specialization classifications may impose a significant condition on their conclusion that diversity enhances urban economic growth.

In addition to the almost exclusive focus upon goods production and distribution, another problem is that the definitions of specialization employed by Glaeser et al. (1992) blurred the critical distinction between *traded* goods and services and *nontraded* goods and services. As I argued in Chapter 2, the traded goods and service industries alone are the sources of expansion or contraction of metropolitan economies. Therefore, if specialization matters, it is only specialization in traded goods and services that could possibly matter.

In the next section, I explain the data set that I have used to analyze the shifting characteristics of metropolitan areas. Then I address the issue of primacy, that is, the extent to which earnings in each of the six traded goods and services groups are concentrated in the top ranked metropolitan areas. I next explain the measure of specialization that I have developed. Using that measure, I then sort the metropolitan areas into those that are specialized in each of the six groups and those that are not for 1969 and 1996.

As one would expect in light of the national shifts documented above, the number of metropolitan areas specialized in goods production and distribution has declined while the number specialized in the information sector has expanded. I also address the question of whether the places that are specialized in information differ from places specialized in goods production and distribution, on many dimensions (size, income level, human capital, and others). Finally, in the last section I examine specialization among the largest (over one million in population) metropolitan areas, and I show that recent population growth in large central cities is characteristic of places specialized in the information sector.

Metropolitan Data

The sample is actually a universe, because it includes all of the metropolitan areas so defined by the U.S. Office of Management and Budget (OMB) as of July 1997. There are 273 metropolitan areas included in the 50 states. That includes all 245 metropolitan statistical areas (MSA), all 17 consolidated metropolitan statistical areas (CMSA), and 11 New England consolidated metropolitan areas (NECMA). An MSA is usually a city with a population of 50,000 or more plus surrounding suburbs. The basic building blocks for MSAs are whole counties (except in New England). Thus, an MSA may be one or more contiguous counties. When two or more contiguous MSAs reach a combined population of one million or more, and there is a minimum threshold of cross-border journeys to work, then the two MSAs are combined into one CMSA.

The source for the metropolitan data used in these definitions is the Regional Economic Information System (REIS) of the Bureau of Economic Analysis (BEA) of the U.S. Department of Commerce. Each year in May, the BEA releases the annual REIS CD; it publishes some of the data in later issues of the *Survey of Current Business*. The REIS includes personal income and its components, population, and earnings for every SIC two-digit industry for every county, metropolitan area, and state, annually from 1969 through 1996 (as of May 1998). Each year the metropolitan area data are reconfigured back to 1969, the first year reported, based on the latest available official OMB definitions of the county composition of MSAs and CMSAs. Thus any one REIS CD has consistent metropolitan definitions (i.e., the county composition is fixed back in time) from 1969 to the present.

The REIS also includes employment data for each metropolitan area. This body of data is more inclusive than any of the other employment data series available annually for places smaller than states. Like the nonagricultural establishment employment series of the Bureau of Labor Statistics (BLS), it is a count of jobs, not employed persons, in the county where the job is located. But it also covers any agriculture, forestry, and fishery jobs; and most importantly, it covers the self-employed, which the BLS series does not cover. The least inclusive annual employment series for areas smaller than states is the Census Bureau's *County Business Patterns*. That series, like the BLS series, is a count of jobs in the county of work, but it excludes not only the self-employed and agricultural, fisheries, and forestry workers, but also all government workers and railroad workers. The differences are not trivial. For the year 1998, U.S. employment reported by *County Business Patterns* was 107 million. For the same year, the BLS reported a national total of 126 million. And the BEA series from the annual REIS was 160 million. Most of the large difference reflects the inclusion of 27 million proprietors. Unless stated otherwise, all references to metropolitan employment here are to the most comprehensive annual data, the REIS series.

The traditional variable utilized in measuring economic performance for areas smaller than states has been employment. The traditional variable utilized in measuring economic performance of the nation or states has been constant dollar output: GDP or GSP (gross state product). Employment data are available for metropolitan areas, gross product data are not, and so analysts have settled for employment data. But in this book I use earnings by industry rather than employment by industry as the basic measure from which metropolitan specialization variables are constructed. Although Gleaser et al. (1992) and Henderson, Kuncoro, and Turner (1995) use industry employment as the basis from which they construct measures of metropolitan specialization, I think that earnings better reflects the importance of an industry for a metropolitan area. Not all jobs are equal in terms of what they add to, or subtract from, a metropolitan economy. For example, the securities industry (SIC code 62, a component of financial producer services) accounted for 7% of employment in Manhattan in 1999, while the health services industry (SIC code 80, a component of advanced consumer services) accounted for 5% (New York State Department of Labor 2000). However, the securities industry accounted for 23% of earnings in Manhattan that year, while the health services industry accounted for less than 4% (BEA 2001a).

Another disadvantage of using employment data as a measure of industry performance over time is that differential growth in productivity across industries may result in opposite movements of employment that do *not* reflect the direction of output growth. For example, if two industries in a metropolitan area each have real output growth (not observable from published data) of 20% over ten years, and the first has productivity growth (output per worker) of 25%, then that industry will show an employment change of about −5%. If the second has zero productivity growth, akin to Baumol's (1967) unprogressive sector, then it will show an employment change of about +20%. Because the metropolitan employment data are observable, while neither output nor productivity data are observable for metropolitan areas, one could make the mistaken inference that the first industry is in decline and the second industry is expanding. Such false inferences were often made in the deindustrialization debate of the 1980s and early 1990s, as I have pointed out elsewhere (Drennan 1996).

A third reason for not using employment data by industry as the basic measure for economic performance of metropolitan areas is that the detailed industry employment data that are available are the least comprehensive, the *County Business Pattern* data from the Census Bureau. The more comprehensive BLS data are not available at the two-digit SIC code level of industry detail that I require. Even if they were, because they omit the self-employed, they are less than comprehensive. Finally, the REIS provides metropolitan employment data that are comprehensive at the metropolitan level just as they are at the national level.

However, they are available only at the one-digit SIC code level, and so those data cannot be used to construct the traded goods and services sectors and their component groups as I have defined them here.

The earnings data from REIS are available at the two-digit level of industry detail for metropolitan areas; they include earnings of the self-employed as well as employees; and earnings is a closer proxy for industry output than is employment. I have included total metropolitan employment from the REIS data as one variable. All of the earnings data have been deflated using the national chain-weighted GDP deflator, (1992 = 100). All of the metropolitan data used in my analysis are from the REIS for 1998, with metropolitan data from 1969 through 1996, with one exception. I have added the percent of adults (aged 25 or older) with a college degree or more by metropolitan area, from the decennial censuses of 1970, 1980, and 1990.

Traded Goods and Services Specializations in Metropolitan Areas, 1969–1996

Primacy

In urban economics, *primacy* refers to the extent to which some national variable, such as population, is concentrated in one or a few urban places. Such concentration is interpreted as indicating the existence of external economies, called agglomeration economies, for that place. "Primacy measures agglomeration at the highest end: the share of the largest employer-city in national own-industry employment" (Black and Henderson 1999, p. 324). One initial issue is whether the six groups of traded goods and services industries that I have designated as specializations are in fact too broad to capture anything unique about sets of metropolitan areas. Black and Henderson (1999) measure primacy using employment in detailed manufacturing industries. The percent share of national employment in that industry in the place with the most jobs in that industry is their measure of primacy.

I have computed real earnings (1992 dollars) in each of the six traded goods and services groups for each of the 273 metropolitan areas, for 1969 and 1996. I have ranked the places from largest earnings in the group to smallest. The number one place and the top ten places represent my measure of primacy. As a standard, I also ranked the 273 places on total earnings. The results are summarized

Table 3.2. Measures of Primacy: Percentage of Earnings of First
and Top Ten Metropolitan Areas for All U.S. Earnings and for
Earnings in Specialized Group, 1969 and 1996

	1969	1996
All earnings		
First (New York)	14.0	11.6
Top ten	48.3	45.0
Primary production		
First (L.A. in '69, Houston in '96)	5.2	11.0
Top ten	26.0	37.5
Manufacturing		
First (New York)	12.9	8.2
Top ten	50.2	43.3
Distribution		
First (New York)	16.7	11.2
Top ten	50.2	45.4
Financial producer services		
First (New York)	22.9	23.4
Top ten	55.8	55.8
Other producer services		
First (New York)	20.6	14.2
Top ten	58.1	54.0
Advanced consumer services		
First (New York)	15.1	12.5
Top ten	52.4	45.4

Source: BEA 1998a.

in Table 3.2. (The top ten places for total earnings and for each of the six groups, 1969 and 1996, are in "Supplementary Tables" [2002, Tables S3–S9].)

In 1969, the top ten places ranked on total earnings accounted for 48% of all metropolitan earnings. All of the specialization groups, except primary production, had somewhat larger shares of earnings in their respective specializations concentrated in the top ten places (not necessarily the same ten places as for total earnings). Manufacturing and distribution earnings in the top ten places are 50% of such earnings, close to the 48% of all earnings. Advanced consumer services earnings in the top ten places are 52% of such earnings. The two producer service groups, financial and other, have much higher shares of those earnings in the top ten places: 56% and 58% respectively. That indicates that producer services are more concentrated in the larger places. Henderson (1988) found that specialization in finance and business services tended to rise with metropolitan population size. The low concentration of the primary production group is not surprising given the nature of those activities.

In 1996, top ten places' share of total earnings was somewhat lower: 45% instead of 48%. It is remarkable that the concentration of earnings in the ten top places has been so stable over one-quarter century. The three groups that had been somewhat higher in their top ten earnings concentration, manufacturing, distribution, and advanced consumer services, all had declines and were either at or slightly under the 45% share of all earnings. Thus, earnings in those groups became more diffused than before. The financial producer services group continued to be as concentrated in the top ten as before, with 56% of those earnings in the top ten places. The top ten places of the other producer services group dropped in share from 58% to 54%. Thus, by 1996, the top ten places of the two producer services groups continued to be characterized by greater primacy than the other groups.

In all groups except primary production, the first ranked place is always the New York CMSA, the largest of all the metropolitan areas. The primacy of New York diminishes over time in total earnings and in every group except financial producer services. Financial producer services is also the group in which the primacy of New York is most pronounced, with 23% of financial producer service earnings in both years (see Table 3.2). Note that for 1996, New York's share of earnings in the manufacturing and distribution groups is below its share of all earnings: 11.6%. At the same time, New York's share of earnings in the three groups of the information sector (financial, other producer services, and advanced consumer services) is in each case above its share of all earnings.

With the exception of the primary production group, the top ten places ranked by total earnings are almost always the same ten places ranked by earnings of each group in both 1969 and 1996. (See "Supplementary Tables" 2002, Tables S3–S9.) For 1969, New York, Los Angeles, and Chicago are always first, second, and third, although Chicago rather than Los Angeles is second in distribution. Beyond third place the ranks jump around a good deal. The pattern is similar for 1996. The set of top ten places and their ranks in total earnings did change from 1969 to 1996. Detroit fell from fourth to eighth place, San Francisco and Boston moved up a few ranks, Pittsburgh and Cleveland dropped out of the top ten, and Dallas and Houston were added to the top ten. Nonetheless, the data indicate that primacy, measured by earnings, is very stable over time. It also appears that for manufacturing, distribution, and advanced consumer services the concentration of those earnings in the top ten places has become almost equal to the concentration of all earnings (and they are mostly the same ten places); and so, in respect to primacy, there is nothing unique about those specializations. Although the top ten financial producer services and other producer service places are also mostly the same ten places in terms of total earnings, they differ in having much higher concentrations of their respective earnings.

Relative Specialization

What does it mean to say that an urban area is "specialized" in some economic activity? The traditional measure of urban specialization is the location quotient, which is the ratio of the urban area's employment share in an industry to the national employment share in that industry, that is,

$$LQ_{ij} = (E_{ij}/E_i)/(E_{USj}/E_{US})$$

where E_{ij} is employment in industry j in place i and E_i is total employment in place i. E_{USj} is national employment in industry j and E_{US} is total national employment. A location quotient larger than one indicates greater relative specialization in the industry in that place than in the nation. The assumption is that the national share in any industry is somehow typical, or an average. But if it is an average, then there is a distribution of location quotients for any one industry. If a location quotient greater than one indicates specialization, then roughly half of all urban places are "specialized" in that industry, that is, the upper half of the distribution is above the mean location quotient value of one. I think that that is much too inclusive a criterion for identifying relative specialization. It lumps together the numerous places with location quotients between say 1.01 and 1.40 with the few places with location quotients above 2.00. A better method, which zeroes in on a high order of specialization, is to include only the upper tail of the distribution. Assuming that each distribution of location quotients is roughly normal, then if we define the upper tail as those places with location quotients at or above the mean (1) plus one standard deviation, that would include roughly the top 17% of places. (Recall that 66% of the observations in a normal distribution are within + or − one standard deviation, and so the upper tail and the lower tail each include 17% of the observations.) But there is no need to use location quotients, because they normalize the share with respect to the nation. Roughly 20% of the nation's economic activity, measured by earnings, is accounted for by nonmetropolitan territory. The object here is to compare a metropolitan area with all metropolitan areas, not with the nation. I have devised a measure of relative specialization that uses a metropolitan average rather than a national average and only includes the upper tail of the distribution of the relative specialization measure. For the reasons noted above in the section on data, I use earnings rather than employment in constructing my measure of relative specialization.

For place i ($i = 1$ to 273) to be classified as specialized in group j ($j = 1$ to 6), then

$$(E_{ij}/E_i) \geq (\bar{X}_j + SD_j),$$

where E_{ij}/E_i is earnings in group j in place i as a percent of all earnings in place i, the relative share. $\bar{X}_j$ is the simple mean of the shares of group j for all places, and SD_j is the standard deviation. If a metropolitan area's relative share of earnings in a group is equal to or larger than the mean plus one standard deviation for all metropolitan areas, then it is deemed to be specialized in that group. Employing that criterion, some metropolitan areas have no specialization—they may be said to have diverse economies—while others have more than one specialization. The criterion is not static. Given the shifts in composition of national output noted in Chapter 2, the value for the term $(\bar{X}_j + SD_j)$ has changed for each group j, and the number of places that meet the criterion has also changed.

The distributions for which $\bar{X}_j$ and SD_j are parameters clearly change over time. What remains fixed in my analysis is that only those places that lie in the upper tail of the distribution of relative shares are classified as specialized. Table 3.3 presents the simple means of relative earnings shares and their standard deviations for each of the six traded goods and services groups, for all 273 metropolitan areas, and for the two years 1969 and 1996. Simple means are used because weighted means primarily reflect the group composition of the very largest places, and thus are not typical. As noted in the section on primacy, the ten largest metropolitan areas account for almost half of all the earnings among the 273 metropolitan places. Note that, although the criterion for specialization remains fixed (share $\geq \bar{X}_j + SD_j$), the values do indeed change over time. They change in accordance with the national shifts noted in Chapter 2. The three goods production and distribution groups all show declines in their mean shares and their standard deviations, and so their minimum shares of earnings for classification as specialized also decline. The biggest change among the goods production and

Table 3.3. Relative Specialization Percentages for Metropolitan Areas, 1969 and 1996

	Primary Production	Manufacturing	Distribution	Financial Producer Services	Other Producer Services	Advanced Consumer Services
Mean share of earnings						
1969	5.27	25.13	9.11	4.50	4.95	5.81
1996	3.03	18.82	8.86	5.88	9.89	11.95
Standard deviation						
1969	5.38	14.11	3.71	2.11	2.55	2.10
1996	4.24	10.24	3.03	2.82	3.95	3.42
Minimum share of earnings for classification as specialized (mean + SD)						
1969	10.65	39.24	12.82	6.61	7.50	7.91
1996	7.27	29.06	11.89	8.70	13.84	15.37

Source: Computed from BEA 1998a.

distribution groups is in manufacturing, where the minimum share for specialization dropped from 39% in 1969 to 29% in 1996. The opposite is the case for the three groups of the information sector. In the information sector, other producer services and advanced consumer services show large upward changes in the minimum shares of earnings required for classification as specialized. They rose from under 8% in 1969 to 14% and 15% respectively in 1996. The minimum share for financial producer services only moved from under 7% to under 9%. (The lists of metropolitan areas that are specialized in each of the six groups, for 1969 and 1996, are presented in "Supplementary Tables" [2002, Tables S10–S21].)

Differences among Specialized and Nonspecialized Places

Do places that are classified as specialized in any of the six groups exhibit characteristics that set them apart from all places, from nonspecialized places, and from each other? Characteristics of the six groups of specialized places are summarized in Table 3.4. In order not to muddy the comparisons, places with two or more specializations (and there are many such places) appear in only one group. The criterion for determining in which group to classify such places was their highest Z score, that is,

$$Z_i = (X_{ij} - \bar{X}_j)/SD_j,$$

where X_{ij} is the relative share of earnings in place i in group j, $\bar{X}_j$ is the simple mean relative share of group j for all places, and SD_j is the standard deviation.

If the distributions of relative earnings share for the six groups and two years are approximately normal, then I would expect that the number of places classified as specialized would be around 46 (the upper tail cut off at the mean plus one standard deviation would be 17% of the 273 observations, or 46). Note that only the number of manufacturing places is close to 46. That in part reflects the elimination of overlaps (places with more than one specialization). The manufacturing group had the fewest number of places with some other specialization. I had anticipated that there would be many places specialized in both manufacturing and distribution, but that was not the case. I take up the interesting issue of overlaps in a later section of this chapter.

In both years about two-thirds of the 273 places are classified as specialized. However, the number of places in each group, with one exception, changed markedly from 1969 to 1996. Reflecting the national shift to a relatively smaller goods production and distribution sector, the number of specialized places in each of the three groups in that sector declined. The primary production group dropped from 30 to 20 specialized places. Fifty-three places were specialized in manufacturing in 1969, with aggregate population of 25 million and aggregate earnings of $324 billion. In 1996, 42 places were specialized in manufacturing with absolutely lower population, 20 million, and earnings, $310 billion. The distribution group shows a similar pattern of fewer specialized places (from 35 to 27), less aggregate population, and less aggregate earnings from 1969 to 1996. The financial producer services group is the only one that had the same number of specialized places, 22, in both years. The aggregate population in the places specialized in finance jumped from 29 million to 42 million, and earnings doubled, from $397 billion in 1969 to $798 billion in 1996. That does not reflect extraordinary growth in a fixed set of places, because many of the 22 places included in 1996 were not among the 22 in 1969. Five of the 22 specialized places in 1969 had populations above one million, whereas 8 had populations above one million in 1996. (The lists of places specialized in each group for each year, ranked by their relative share of earnings in the specialization, are shown in "Supplementary Tables" [2002, Tables S10–S21].) The biggest increase is in the number of places specialized in other producer services, which rose from 12 to 29. Their aggregate population went from 12 million to 75 million and their aggregate earnings jumped from $167 billion to $1,343 billion. Although the num-

Table 3.4. Metropolitan Area Characteristics, by Traded Goods and Services Specialization, 1969 and 1996

	PRM	MFG	DIST	PSFIN	PSOTH	ACS	Not Specialized	All Places
Number of metropolitan areas								
1969	30	53	35	22	12	19	102	273
1996	20	42	27	22	29	33	100	273
Median population (thousands)								
1969	142	245	307	311	222	131	155	171
1996	238	267	254	684	1,308	150	184	254
Aggregate population (millions)								
1969	5.2	25.3	28.8	29.3	11.9	18.5	41.2	158.1
1996	6.0	19.7	21.6	42.1	74.9	10.9	36.5	211.8
Aggregate earnings (billions 1992 $)								
1969	50.7	323.7	371.2	397.2	166.9	242.2	479.1	2,005.4
1996	71.2	309.6	355.1	798.3	1,342.8	145.0	510.2	3,531.5
Per capita personal income (1992 $, simple mean)								
1969	12,154	13,949	13,406	14,690	14,679	14,035	12,488	13,222
1996	17,636	19,857	20,262	23,828	22,378	19,384	18,634	19,821
Simple earnings per capita (1992 $)								
1969	9,516	11,873	11,151	11,177	12,229	11,088	10,374	10,682
1996	11,741	14,430	14,905	17,078	16,635	12,265	13,069	13,971
Percentage college graduates								
1970	9.6	8.6	11.1	12.8	15.6	11.8	12.1	11.2
1990	15.8	16.1	19.2	23.5	25.9	18.0	19.8	19.6

Group earnings, specialized places (billion 1992 $)							
1969	8.7	145.2	54.6	36.6	15.6	21.7	NA	NA
1996	10.7	107.2	50.2	116.1	246.6	24.7	NA	NA
Group earnings, all places (billion 1992 $)							
1969	46.5	574.4	216.3	117.7	131.3	124.4	NA	NA
1996	59.5	610.6	356.7	316.8	521.2	405.6	NA	NA
Group earnings of specialized places as percentages of group earnings, all places							
1969	18.7	25.3	25.2	31.1	11.9	17.4	NA	NA
1996	18.0	17.6	14.1	36.6	47.3	6.1	NA	NA
Percentage of personal income from dividends, interest, and rent							
1969	13.3	12.4	13.0	18.9	13.1	15.0	12.5	13.3
1996	16.4	16.8	16.6	19.7	17.7	19.7	17.3	17.6
Percentage of personal income from proprietors' income							
1969	16.5	9.4	10.4	11.0	11.0	11.4	10.3	11.0
1996	11.2	5.9	8.1	6.9	7.8	7.3	7.1	7.4
Percentage of personal income from transfer payments							
1969	11.7	8.3	8.8	9.5	8.8	10.2	9.7	9.5
1996	20.9	17.3	16.8	14.3	14.7	21.2	18.9	18.0

Source: Computed from Regional Economic Information System data.
Note: No metropolitan area appears in more than one category.

ber of places specialized in advanced consumer services rose a good deal, their aggregate population and earnings declined substantially.

In 1969, the median population for places specialized in manufacturing, distribution, and the two producer service groups, were quite similar, ranging from 222,000 to 311,000. By 1996, however, the medians had diverged. The median for manufacturing was about the same (267,000); for distribution it was lower; and for the two producer services groups it was much higher. Indeed, the median population of places specialized in other producer services increased from 222,000 to 1,308,000.

It has long been argued that similar firms clustered in an urban area gain economies that are external to the firm (Marshall 1890; Arrow 1962; Chinitz 1961; Roemer 1986; and Porter 1990). Such external economies include knowledge spillovers favored by proximity in space, and sharing a common pool of laborers skilled in the industry. Those external economies, or agglomeration economies, are tied not so much to the size of the urban area but rather to the degree of specialization. They are labeled agglomeration economies of localization in the urban literature. There are other external or agglomeration economies tied to the size of the urban area. They would include the quality of air service, of cultural amenities, and of health and education services. They are labeled agglomeration economies of urbanization. The observed marked divergence in median size suggests that agglomeration economies became greater for large places specialized in finance, and especially for those specialized in other producer services, but remained unchanged for places specialized in manufacturing and distribution. Assuming that median population of specialized places indicates something about agglomeration economies associated with specialization, then in 1969 the efficient size for a place specialized in manufacturing or distribution was about the same as for places specialized in either producer service group. But in 1996, the inferred efficient size of the producer service places was 2.5 to 5 times larger than the efficient size of the manufacturing or distribution places. This, of course, is not proof or evidence of changing agglomeration economies; rather it is suggestive of such changes. And it is contrary to the argument put forth by the geographers Scott and Storper (1986) regarding manufacturing places: "The more [urban industrial complexes] expand (up to a certain point at least) the more such complexes become attractive as centers of profitable commodity production by reason of their increasing external economies" (p. 304).

The per capita personal income of the two producer service group places was somewhat higher than that in the manufacturing or distribution places in 1969, and the growth to 1996 is greater. That may be an artifact of larger size. Larger metropolitan areas tend to have higher per capita incomes. Also, given that the comparison is not for the identical set of places across time, it is not clear what information such a comparison of growth conveys.

Perhaps the most interesting fact that emerges from Table 3.4 is the opposite trends in concentration. The diminished importance of places specialized in manufacturing and in distribution for all manufacturing and distribution in metropolitan areas is clear. The 53 places specialized in manufacturing in 1969 accounted for 25% of all metropolitan earnings in manufacturing, but the 42 manufacturing places in 1996 accounted for only 18%. The same diminished concentration occurred among the places specialized in distribution. Exactly the opposite occurred in the two producer service groups. The 22 financial producer service places accounted for 31% of all metropolitan earnings in that group in 1969 and 37% in 1996. The other producer services group accounted for only 12% of earnings in that group in 1969 but 47% in 1996. On the other hand, the last group of the information sector, advanced consumer services, followed the deconcentration route of manufacturing and distribution, only more so. From 17% of group earnings in 1969, the places specialized in advanced consumer services went down to 6% in 1996.

The data indicate that over the past quarter-century, manufacturing and distribution have become less concentrated in places specialized in those two groups, while the two producer services have become more concentrated in places specialized in those groups. The view that the information age, specifically the advances in telecommunication, will make urban concentrations irrelevant anachronisms (Toffler 1980; Naisbitt 1994; Negroponte 1995; and Knobe 1996) is called into question by the observed trends. The two producer services groups, while growing faster nationally than the three goods production and distribution groups, have become more concentrated in urban places specialized in producer services, and those places are much larger now than the set of places so specialized in 1969. That finding about two parts of the information sector, the sector in which information is a key input and output, is in accord with a recent analysis by Gaspar and Glaeser (1998) in which they note, "Our empirical work suggests that telecommunications may be a complement to, or at least not a strong substitute for, cities and face-to-face interactions" (p. 136). That is not to assert that the future could not bring dispersion, as it has to manufacturing, distribution, and advanced consumer services. As Capello (1994) has argued, the connection between the technology-driven information economy and the spatial organization of production is complex and uncertain.

Table 3.4 shows the simple means of earnings per capita in each set of places. As is the case with per capita personal income, comparisons of growth over time are fraught with problems of interpretation, because the places included in each group changed from 1969 to 1996. However the earnings per capita data can be analyzed to determine if specialization is associated with different levels of per capita earnings. The same could be done with per capita income, but this is a better measure for my purposes, because earnings per capita represents economic activity in those places only, whereas per capita income includes sources of income that do not reflect economic activity in those places, namely dividends, interest, and rent, plus transfer payments. In the text table below, per capita earnings for the various sets of places have been converted to index numbers where the index for all metropolitan areas is set equal to 100 in 1969 and 1996.

	1969	1996
Primary production	89.1	84.0
Manufacturing	111.1	103.3
Distribution	104.4	106.7
Financial producer services	104.6	122.2
Other producer services	114.5	119.1
Advanced consumer services	103.8	87.8
Not specialized	97.1	93.5
All metropolitan areas	100.0	100.0
RANGE	89–115	84–122

For 1969, all specialized sets of places except the primary production set have per capita earnings above the metropolitan average, while the set of nonspecialized places is below the metropolitan average. For 1996, however, the set of advanced consumer services places falls well below the metropolitan average; manufacturing and distribution places continue to be above, but close to, the metropolitan average; and financial and other producer service places have the highest values, about 20% above the mean. Note that in both years the nonspecialized places are below the metropolitan average. It is not clear if the pattern exhibited is tied to specialization or to population size (the nonspecialized place and the advanced consumer services places are smaller than the others, based on median population). Both Glaeser et al. (1992) and Quigley (1998) have argued that diversity, not specialization, promote population and income growth. These data do not prove otherwise, but they are suggestive of the opposite about income. I take this issue up in the next chapter.

The per capita earnings data are also suggestive about the issue of income convergence. The neoclassical model of income growth argues that incomes of different regions, states, and metropolitan areas will tend to converge in the long run, because of the mobility of labor and capital. The most thorough recent analysis of that issue, by Barro and Sala-I-Martin (1991), found that in ten-year intervals over the past hundred years, states' per capita incomes have indeed converged. The exceptions they noted are the decades of the 1920s and the 1980s, which they dismiss as the products of unusual events. Others have found evidence of income divergence in the 1980s (Carlino 1992; Drennan, Tobier, and Lewis 1996; Garnick 1990) for both states and metropolitan areas. In a recent article that I wrote with José Lobo (1999), we found evidence of divergence, the opposite of convergence, for metropolitan areas. Our data ended in 1995. The question remaining unanswered is, Was the divergence in per capita incomes of the 1980s a one-time fluke, as Barro and Sala-I-Martin contend, or was it the beginning of a new pattern that has continued in the 1990s? The data above very roughly suggest divergence, because the range of the index numbers has widened markedly, from 89–115 in 1969 to 84–122 in 1996. Also, two sets of places below the mean in 1969 (primary production and nonspecialized) were further below the mean in 1996. Two other sets of places above the mean in 1969 (financial and other producer services) had become much more above the mean in 1996. I emphasize that this is only suggestive, because it may be an artifact of population size. Recall that the upward diverging sets of places, the two producer service groups, had become much larger in 1996. I address this issue of income convergence or divergence in Chapter 5.

The specialized places differ markedly on one other measure, the percentage of adults (over age 24) with at least a college degree. The average for all metropolitan places was 11% in 1970 and almost 20% in 1990. The distribution places and the advanced consumer services places are very close to the metropolitan average for both years. The primary production and manufacturing places are below the metropolitan average for both years. In 1990 financial producer services places had a mean college attainment of 24%, and for other producer services the mean was 26%. That is not surprising given the occupational distribution in the two producer service groups. Both have much higher proportions of managerial and professional jobs than the primary production, manufacturing, and distribution groups, as noted in Chapter 1 (see Table 1.1) and as demonstrated by Beyers (1992).

Other measures on Table 3.4 do not show a strong difference among the sets of metropolitan areas. The share of personal income from proprietors' income, a crude measure of entrepreneurial activity, does not vary much across the groups. It is unusually high in the primary production group, perhaps reflecting farm proprietors. The share of income from transfer payments, a crude measure of dependency, does exhibit some variation. The highest share, in 1996, 21%, is registered in the primary production group and in the advanced consumer services group. Note that they also have the lowest levels of per capita earnings for that year. The two producer services groups have the lowest shares of income from transfer payments for 1996, 14% to 15% compared with the average for all metropolitan areas of 18%. The manufacturing and distribution places have shares that are also below the metropolitan average, but less so. Shares of income from dividends, interest, and rent hardly vary across the groups.

The data shown for the 100 or so places that are classified as not specialized indicate that they tend to be small, with median populations of less than 200,000; to have below average per capita income and per capita earnings; and to have college education means about equal to the metropolitan average. Further, over time there has been no rise in either the number of nonspecialized places or in their collective concentration of population and earnings. Although some specializations are in decline, specialization, as defined here, is clearly not in decline among metropolitan areas.

Specialization among Large Metropolitan Areas

The section above on primacy shows that absolute earnings in five of the six traded goods and services groups in 1996 were highly concentrated (43% to

56%) in the ten top ranked places, ranked by absolute earnings in the group (see Table 3.2). In the section above on relative specialization, nothing is conveyed about the size of specialized places other than median population, because my measure of specialization is relative rather than absolute. Here I examine the extent to which large metropolitan areas (with populations of one million or more) are specialized, if they have more than one specialization and if they tend to be specialized in certain traded goods and services groups rather than others.

In 1969, there were 33 metropolitan areas with populations of one million or more. Of those, 23 were specialized and 10 were not. In 1996, the number of large metropolitan areas was 46. All but 8 of them were specialized, as shown below. Clearly, specialization is a feature of large metropolitan areas, and more so in 1996 than it had been in 1969.

	1969	1996
3 specializations	0	3
2 specializations	1	14
1 specialization	22	21
0 specializations	10	8
All large places	33	46

Not only are the great majority of the 46 large metropolitan areas of 1996 specialized, but 17 of them are specialized in more than one group compared with only one place with more than one specialization for 1969. (Recall that for Table 3.4 places with more than one specialization were deleted from all groups except that one in which their specialization was greatest.) The 46 metropolitan areas with populations of one million or more in 1996 are listed in rank order by population in Table 3.5. Their number of specializations, zero to three, is indicated as well as the group or groups in which they are specialized and the percent share of their earnings from that group. Three of them, Atlanta, Dallas, and Miami, are specialized in three groups: distribution, financial producer services, and other producer services. The most common pairing of specializations is of the two producer service groups. There are 10 such pairs. And those pairs occur among places with populations above 2.2 million. The second most common pairing is distribution with financial producer services, which occurs in six places. Among the 46 large places, there is only one specialized in the primary

Table 3.5. Metropolitan Areas with Populations of One Million or More and Their Specializations, 1996

Rank	Large Metropolitan Area	Population 1996	Number of Specializations	Percentage of Earnings in Group					
				PRMSH	MFGSH	DISTSH	PSFINISH	PSOTHSH	ACSSH
1	New York, NY-NJ-CT-PA (CMSA)	19,800	2				18.12	18.05	
2	Los Angeles, CA (CMSA)	15,427	1					16.59	
3	Chicago, IL-IN-WI (CMSA)	8,590	2				10.35	17.32	
4	Washington, DC-MD-VA-WV (CMSA)	7,146	1					22.57	
5	San Francisco, CA (CMSA)	6,616	1					21.47	
6	Philadelphia, PA-NJ-DE-MD (CMSA)	5,973	2				9.58	13.94	
7	Boston, MA-NH (NECMA)	5,788	2				10.21	17.85	
8	Detroit, MI (CMSA)	5,423	1		34.20				
9	Dallas, TX (CMSA)	4,565	3			14.41	9.49	15.05	
10	Houston, TX (CMSA)	4,240	2	7.99				15.99	
11	Atlanta, GA (MSA)	3,531	3			16.83	8.90	20.41	
12	Miami, FL (CMSA)	3,478	3			14.42	9.86	15.55	
13	Seattle, WA (CMSA)	3,309	1					18.00	
14	Cleveland, OH (CMSA)	2,909	0						
15	Minneapolis, MN-WI (MSA)	2,760	2			13.06	10.00		
16	Phoenix, AZ (MSA)	2,753	2				10.08	14.41	
17	San Diego, CA (MSA)	2,677	1					17.35	
18	St. Louis, MO-IL (MSA)	2,548	0						
19	Pittsburgh, PA (MSA)	2,374	1						16.13
20	Denver, CO (CMSA)	2,272	2				8.70	21.52	
21	Tampa, FL (MSA)	2,199	2				9.48	18.31	
22	Portland, OR-WA (CMSA)	2,073	1			12.37			
23	Cincinnati, OH-KY-IN (CMSA)	1,919	1			12.53			

24	Kansas City, MO-KS (MSA)	1,688	2			12.77		15.86	
25	Milwaukee, WI (CMSA)	1,638	0					13.86	
26	Sacramento, CA (CMSA)	1,631	1						
27	Norfolk, VA-NC (MSA)	1,536	0						
28	Indianapolis, IN (MSA)	1,489	1				8.83		
29	San Antonio, TX (MSA)	1,486	0						
30	Columbus, OH (MSA)	1,447	1				10.92		
31	Orlando, FL (MSA)	1,426	2			16.10		16.15	
32	Charlotte, NC-SC (MSA)	1,319	2				10.36		16.14
33	New Orleans, LA (MSA)	1,308	1					14.70	
34	Salt Lake City, UT (MSA)	1,226	1			12.11			
35	Las Vegas, NV-AZ (MSA)	1,198	0						
36	Buffalo, NY (MSA)	1,173	0						
37	Greensboro, NC (MSA)	1,139	1		29.53				
38	Nashville, TN (MSA)	1,114	2					13.98	
39	Hartford, CT (NECMA)	1,106	1				16.62		
40	Rochester, NY (MSA)	1,086	1		34.60				15.94
41	Memphis, TN-AR-MS (MSA)	1,075	1			20.71		17.54	
42	Austin, TX (MSA)	1,041	1					16.85	
43	Raleigh, NC (MSA)	1,022	1						
44	Oklahoma City, OK (MSA)	1,022	0		35.13				
45	Grand Rapids, MI (MSA)	1,015	1			13.30	12.91		
46	Jacksonville, FL (MSA)	1,015	2						
	Minimum share for specialization			7.27	29.06	11.89	8.70	13.84	15.37

Source: BEA 1998a.
Note: Only principal city of each metropolitan area is shown; full name includes surrounding cities.

production group, Houston, and there are only three specialized in advanced consumer services. Only four of the large places are specialized in manufacturing (Detroit, Greensboro, Rochester, N.Y., and Grand Rapids) and those four do not have any other specializations. The most common specialization of the large places is other producer services. Half of the places are specialized in other producer services. Note that all but one (Detroit) of the 13 largest places are specialized in other producer services. But even Detroit is close to the minimum threshold, 13.84%, for specialization in other producer services with a share of 12.45%. Seven of the 12 largest places are specialized in financial producer services.

Black and Henderson (1999) note that financial and business services and high-tech services tend to be concentrated in the largest metropolitan areas. The data for 1996 certainly confirm that, but the data for 1969 indicate that that was not always the case. As shown below, only seven of the 33 large places were specialized in financial and other producer services in 1969, while 14 were specialized in manufacturing and distribution.

	1969	1996
Primary production	0	1
Manufacturing	5	4
Distribution	9	11
Financial producer services	5	16
Other producer services	2	23
Advanced consumer services	2	3

Similarly the median population of places specialized in financial and producer services ranged from 0.2 to 0.3 million in 1969 but jumped to 0.7 to 1.3 million in 1996 (see Table 3.4). Large size has not always been characteristic of metropolitan areas specialized in financial and other producer services, as Noyelle and Stanback (1984) first noted. Sassen (1991) summarizes the findings of Noyelle and Stanback regarding specialization among the 140 largest metropolitan areas. "The larger the SMSA, the greater the weight of producer services compared with distributive services. It should be noted that the larger SMSAs, were once predominantly centers for the production and export of manufacturing" (p. 157).

The list of large places and their specializations in 1996 provides a reality check on our perceptions or preconceptions about American urban areas. Seven places on the list have traditionally been viewed as manufacturing places. They are, in order of size, Chicago, Philadelphia, Cleveland, Pittsburgh, Milwaukee, Indianapolis, and Buffalo. By the criterion used here, none of them are specialized in manufacturing. The largest one, Chicago, is not even close to specialization in manufacturing. Its share of earnings in manufacturing is 20%, a tad higher than the mean manufacturing share for all metropolitan places, 19%. Chicago is highly specialized in financial and other producer services and comes quite close to specialization in distribution too (it is less than one percentage point below the minimum share of 12%). Given the trends in the national economy, that kind of economic base is not a bad thing for Chicago. Not everyone has noticed the change in Chicago's economy. In her book, *New York, Chicago, Los Angeles: America's Global Cities* (1999) Janet Abu-Lughod notes that manufacturing employment in the city of Chicago dropped from 668,000 in 1947 to 187,000 in 1992 and that it also fell for the entire metropolitan area, but much less so. She asserts that "the lack of federal defense contracts, particularly in R & D, was largely to blame for [Chicago's] manufacturing losses" (p. 325). I would venture, rather, that productivity growth in manufacturing, resulting in a need for less labor per unit of output, and the litany of established factors that pulled manufacturing out of all big cities are "largely to blame." She concludes the section on Chicago by noting, "In the short run, the picture looks dim indeed, as de-industrialization and international restructuring remove more and more of the city's traditional economic underpinnings" (p. 356). I would argue that the traditional economic underpinnings have been replaced by far better underpinnings.

Growth and Decline of Large Central Cities

One aspect of metropolitan performance not touched upon in this chapter is the economic condition of the major city, the central city, in the metropolitan area. The best single barometer of economic condition of a city is population change. Cities with declining populations are cities in distress. In their careful analysis of economic and fiscal condition of American cities, Ladd and Yinger (1989) demonstrate that large cities (populations of 500,000 or more) had much worse fiscal condition than smaller cities in 1982. Their data show that two out of three large cities experienced population losses in the 1970s. Thus, population loss among large cities is associated with poor fiscal health.

Among the central cities of the 46 largest (over one million population) metropolitan areas in the twenty years from 1970 to 1990, cities losing population (25) outnumbered cities gaining population (21). The phenomenon of the shrinking big city and its attendant ills has been a staple of urban journalism and urban studies classrooms for at least a quarter-century. However, the pattern of more big cities losing population than gaining population was reversed during the 1990s, according to recently released data from the 2000 decennial census. Among the same 46 cities of the largest metropolitan areas, cities gaining population (33) far outnumbered cities losing population (13). In terms of aggregate population, from 1970 to 1990 those 46 cities barely changed. Huge losses in large, old cities of the Northeast and Midwest (New York, Philadelphia, Washington, Chicago, Detroit, Cleveland, and St. Louis) from 1970 to 1990 were offset by gains in newer cities of the Sunbelt (Los Angeles, Dallas, Houston, Phoenix, and San Antonio). In the past decade, however, those 46 cities grew by a collective 3.2 million, a gain of 9 percent. (The individual cities and their populations are listed in the Appendix.)

Many disks have been filled with descriptions of and explanations for the 1970 to 1990 population decline characteristic of many large cities, especially those in the Northeast and the Midwest. For my purpose here, it is the recent decade that is of interest. Are cities that had population growth 1990–2000 different from those that had population decline? In particular, do metropolitan specialization and city size seem to matter for city population growth or decline in the 1990s?

The 33 central cities with population gains from 1990 to 2000 are in metropolitan areas that collectively have 49 specializations (recall that the number of specializations can exceed the number of metropolitan areas because some metropolitan areas have more than one specialization). The 13 central cities with population losses from 1990 to 2000 are in metropolitan areas that collectively have only 9 specializations (Table 3.6). Further, almost half of the 33 cities with population gains are in metropolitan areas with two or even three specializations, whereas only one of the 13 cities with population losses is in a metropolitan area with two specializations. Of the eight large metropolitan areas with no specialization, five of their cities had population losses. Thus, metropolitan spe-

Table 3.6. Number and Type of Specialization in Growing and Declining Central
Cities of Large Metropolitan Areas, 1990–2000

Characteristics of Metropolitan Area	Central Cities with Increasing Population	Central Cities with Declining Population
Number of specializations		
3	3	0
2	13	1
1	14	7
0	3	5
TOTAL	33	13
Type of specialization		
Primary production	1	0
Manufacturing	2	2
Distribution	10	1
Financial producer services	14	2
Other producer services	20	3
Advanced consumer services	2	1
TOTAL	49	9

Source: U.S. Census Bureau 2000.

cialization is more characteristic or more common among cities with increases
in population than among cities with decreases in population. Most interesting
is the preponderance of places specialized in financial and other producer services among cities with gains in population. Similarly, ten of the eleven large
places specialized in distribution have central cities with rising population.

The descriptive data in Table 3.6 give the impression that metropolitan areas
that are more specialized are more likely to have growing central cities than metropolitan areas that are less specialized. Better than impressions are formal statistical tests. I have sorted the 46 cities by two categorical variables: city population increase or decrease, and four metropolitan specialization classifications
that are nonoverlapping, as shown in Table 3.7.

A chi-square test performed with this data indicates that city population gain
or loss is *not* independent of metropolitan specialization (the calculated chi-
square statistic is 10.17, the critical chi-square for the .05 significance level is
7.81).

Does city size matter for the city growth that occurred in the 1990s? Using
the same 46 central cities, the major central city in each of the 46 largest (over
one million population) metropolitan areas, I sorted them by two variables, size
and population gain or loss. Cities with year 2000 population of 500,000 or
more I call large, those below 500,000, small. It looks as if large cities were more

Table 3.7. Number of Growing and Declining Central Cities,
Sorted by Sector of Specialization, 1990–2000

Specialization	Increasing Population	Declining Population
None	3	5
Goods production and distribution only	5	3
Information only	17	5
Mixed specialization	8	0
TOTAL	33	13

Source: Table 3.5 and U.S. Census Bureau 2000.

likely to gain population in the 1990s than small cities (see text table), but formal tests are more reliable than impressions.

	Population Gain	Population Loss	Total
Small cities	12	9	21
Large cities	21	4	25

A chi-square test performed with this data indicates that city population gain or loss is *not* independent of city size (the calculated chi-square statistic is 3.89, the critical chi-square for the .05 significance level is 3.84).

The 1990–2000 population change data for the central city of each large metropolitan area strongly suggest that *metropolitan* specialization favors *city* population growth. Particularly, metropolitan specialization in either producer service group or in distribution appears to favor city population growth. That is not the case for specialization in manufacturing or advanced consumer services. A tentative hypothesis that comports with the data is that the spatial dispersion of manufacturing, outside of cities and outside of metropolitan areas, fosters central city population decline or stagnation. On the other hand, the spatial concentration of financial and other producer services in the downtowns of large cities, a fact that has been established in a number of studies (Mills 1988; Drennan 1992, 2000; Schwartz 1993) fosters city population growth. Metropolitan areas highly specialized in financial or other producer services, or both, are more likely to have economically viable central cities. Apparently, agglomeration economies of localization tend to maintain spatial concentrations of producer services in large cities.

4 | Metropolitan Income and Growth
The Roles of Specialization, Size, and Human Capital

The wealth of descriptive statistics about metropolitan areas presented in Chapter 3 suggests a number of testable propositions that I phrase as questions.

1. Does specialization improve the level of income more than diversity?
2. If so, do some specializations add more to the level of income than others?
3. Is the effect of specialization upon the level of income different in different time periods?
4. Is specialization positively related to metropolitan size?
5. Does the level of human capital positively affect the level of metropolitan income?
6. Do specialization and human capital affect metropolitan income growth?
7. Do size, specialization, and human capital affect metropolitan population growth and metropolitan employment growth?

Most of these are questions about the economic effects of metropolitan specialization. As already noted in Chapter 3, theories favoring specialization as an important source of productivity enhancement have a long history in economics (see Marshall 1890; Schumpeter 1942; Arrow 1962; Roemer 1986; and Porter 1990).

In this chapter I present a formal model developed with my co-authors in an earlier work (Drennan et al. forthcoming) for metropolitan productivity, or output per worker, proxied by real per capita personal income, in which all traded goods and services industries are grouped into the familiar six functional groups. I draw heavily upon our past analysis of the effects of specialization upon the level of income. I have broadened the analysis here, however, to include the effects of all three (specialization, human capital, and size) not only upon metropolitan income and growth but also upon population growth and employment growth. The level and the growth of real per capita personal income and the growth of population and employment are related to specialization, human capital, and size. The model is estimated with cross-section data for 269 metropolitan areas for a few different time periods between 1969 and 1996. I also estimate equations relating relative specialization to absolute metropolitan size. The point of that effort is to investigate more rigorously some of the issues raised in Chapter 3 now stated as questions. In this chapter I first present the model then describe the metropolitan data. I present the estimated equations and evaluate the results. Finally, I address the questions raised in light of the statistical results, and present some concluding points. Readers not interested in formal models and their econometric estimation may skip right to the concluding section of this chapter without losing the threads of argument that I lay out in this book.

Modeling and Estimation Framework

Metropolitan areas are treated as separate economies sharing common pools of labor and capital. Differences in metropolitan economic performance cannot then be accounted for by differences in savings rate, capital-to-labor ratios, or exogenous labor endowments. Given the assumption of mobile labor and capital, metropolitan economies differ only in their level of productivity, that is, output per worker. Total metropolitan output at time t, $Y_{i,t}$, is given by:

$$Y_{it} = A_{it} f(N_{it}) = A_{it} N_{it}^{\alpha}, \tag{4.1}$$

where $A_{i,t}$ represents the location-specific technology of the ith metropolitan area at time t, $N_{i,t}$ denotes metropolitan population at time t, $f(\bullet)$ is a production function common across metropolitan areas and α is an economywide production parameter. A similar type of production function is used by Glaeser, Scheinkman, and Shleifer (1995). Dividing both sides by population yields

$$y_{it} = A_{it} N_{it}^{a-1}, \tag{4.2}$$

where $y_{i,t}$ denotes per capita output. Taking the natural logarithm of (4.2),

$$Iny_{it} = InA_{it} + (\alpha - 1)InN_{it}. \tag{4.3}$$

I hypothesize that metropolitan productivity is an exponential function of location specific characteristics (e.g., specialization in traded goods and service production, educational attainment of the metropolitan labor force, public infrastructure, etc.):

$$A_{it} = \exp\left[\beta_0 + \sum_{m=1}^{M} \beta_m X_{mit}\right] \tag{4.4}$$

where m indexes the number of variables representing the determinants of metropolitan productivity. Inserting equation (4.4) into equation (4.3),

$$Iny_{it} = \beta_0 + \sum_{m=1}^{M} \beta_m X_{mit} + (\alpha - 1)InN_{it} \tag{4.5}$$

Equation (4.5) is the general form of the model. Data limitations restrict the specification of the equations actually estimated in a number of ways. There being no aggregate output data for metropolitan areas, the closest available proxy is personal income. In the equations estimated, the $y_{(it)}$ of equation (4.5) is income per capita rather than output per capita.

The location-specific characteristics that may affect the level of productivity in a place may be many and include such things as public infrastructure, climate, entrepreneurial culture, path dependence, and so on. All are plausible candidates for inclusion in the A term of equation (4.4). I have two location-specific characteristics that I include in my specification and estimation of the A term, namely the six relative specialization measures and the level of human capital, measured by the percent of adults (aged 25 or more) with at least a college degree. The specification of the equation to be estimated, then, is

$$\begin{aligned} y_{(i)} = b_{(0)} + b_{(1)}SH_{(i1)} + \ldots + b_{(6)}SH_{(i6)} + b_{(7)}COLL_{(i)} \\ + (a - 1)\ln N_{(i)} + e_{(i)}, \end{aligned} \tag{4.6}$$

where $y_{(i)}$ is per capita personal income in metropolitan area i, and $SH_{(i1)}$ is relative specialization in traded goods and services group 1 in metropolitan area i, and so on for the six specializations. The variable $COLL_{(i)}$ is the percentage of adults with college or more education in metropolitan area i.

The specification, equation (4.6), provides a test for the effect of location-specific characteristics (specialization and human capital) and size (measured by $N_{(i)}$, population) upon the *level* of income or productivity, not upon the *growth* of income or population. Consequently, I have also estimated equations relating the growth of per capita personal income and the growth of population and employment to initial characteristics, those at the beginning of the time period over which growth is measured. That has become the preferred functional format for estimating growth equations, as Glaeser (1994) has explained so well:

> The advantages of this simple format [regressing growth rates on initial conditions] are great, compared with the complexity of the other possible approaches to testing theories about national, regional, or urban growth. The other literature tends to be much more complicated and has been so for decades. In particular both growth economists and regional economists regularly regressed changes on changes. The changes-on-changes approach is correct only when the researcher is confident of both using the functional form and not omitting any relevant variables. Modern empirical style is more likely to focus on the less dangerous (and less ambitious) simple regressions between later changes and earlier conditions than on the testing of a complex multi-equation structural model. (p. 14)

One of the questions posed above is whether the degree of specialization is positively related to the size of metropolitan areas. That question is prompted by the data of Tables 3.4 and 3.5, which suggest that the median sizes of places with some specializations are markedly higher than the median sizes of places with other specializations or with no specializations. It also suggests that large places, one million or more in population, are more likely to be specialized, than smaller places. To answer that question, the following equation has been estimated.

$$SH_{(ik)} = a_{(0)} + a_{(1)}POP_{(i)} + a_{(2)}POP^2_{(i)} + e_{(ik)} \qquad (4.7)$$

Where $SH_{(ik)}$ is the relative share of earnings in metropolitan area i and specialization k ($k = 1$ to 6), $POP_{(i)}$ is the population of place i, and $POP^2_{(i)}$ is the population squared. If $a_{(1)} > 0$, and $a_{(2)} < 0$, then the share rises with population to some maximum where the derivative, $dSH_{(ik)}/dPOP_{(i)} = 0$. Henderson (1988) estimated a similar equation for his relative share measures for metropolitan areas and found quite different maximum sizes at which specialization peaked.

Data and Variable Description

The original sample, or universe, used in the analysis in Chapter 3 consists of the 273 MSAs (metropolitan statistical areas), CMSAs, (consolidated metropolitan statistical areas), and NECMAs (New England consolidated metropolitan areas) as defined by the Office of Management and Budget as of July 1997 and as described in Chapter 3. Here the number of metropolitan areas is reduced by four to 269. The four dropped from the sample are all small places that were not classified as metropolitan areas at the time of the 1990 decennial census. Consequently, I was not able to obtain the college completion variable, which is from the census, for those places.

As explained in Chapter 3, I have computed the relative share of earnings in each of the six traded goods and services groups for the four years 1969, 1979, 1989, and 1996 and for each metropolitan area. I must emphasize that the regression equations estimated and presented below are always for the entire sample of places, not for subsets of places deemed as highly specialized in some group by the criterion laid out in Chapter 3.

The descriptive statistics for all of the variables used in this analysis, for the 269 metropolitan areas and for the four years are listed in Table 4.1, along with definitions of those variables. Per capita personal income varies a good deal among the metropolitan areas. The maximum is more than three times larger than the minimum in most of the years shown.

Note that the minimum population is tiny for 1969. That reflects the fact that some of the places presently classified as metropolitan areas were too small to be so classified back in 1969. The percentage of adults with at least college degrees (COLL) rose from a metropolitan average of 11.2% in 1970 to 19.6% in 1990. The coefficient of variation (standard deviation/mean) for the college variable dropped from 0.35 to 0.31, indicating less variability in that measure among metropolitan areas. Although Glaeser, Scheinkman, and Shleifer (1995) used two additional measures of human capital (the percentage of adults with 12 to 15 years of education, and median years of schooling), I think that the college completion rate is a better measure for my purposes. First, it shows much greater variability among metropolitan areas than does years of schooling. The coefficient of variation for average years of schooling among metropolitan areas was

Table 4.1. Descriptive Statistics and Definitions for Metropolitan Variables
(n = 269)

Variable	1969	1979	1989	1996
PCPI[a] (1992 $)				
Mean	13,254	16,391	18,476	19,869
Standard deviation	2,196	2,541	3,162	3,227
Maximum	20,996	25,945	31,038	34,044
Minimum	6,786	9,114	9,516	10,261
Coefficient of variation	0.17	0.16	0.17	0.16
POP[b] (thousands)				
Mean	587	652	729	786
Standard deviation	1,578	1,624	1,779	1,865
Maximum	19,264	18,857	19,491	19,800
Minimum	26	55	57	57
Coefficient of variation	2.69	2.49	2.44	2.37
COLL[c] (percentages)				
Mean	11.2	16.5	19.6	—
Standard deviation	3.9	5.2	6.0	—
Maximum	27.4	38.6	44.0	—
Minimum	5.1	7.7	9.5	—
Coefficient of variation	0.35	0.31	0.31	—
PRMSH[d] (percentages)				
Mean	5.2	4.5	3.4	3.0
Standard deviation	5.4	5.2	4.3	4.3
Maximum	31.3	30.4	24.6	26.6
Minimum	0.7	0.4	0.4	0.2
Coefficient of variation	1.03	1.17	1.24	1.41
MFGSH[e] (percentages)				
Mean	25.3	24.4	20.8	18.9
Standard deviation	14.1	13.0	11.0	10.3
Maximum	61.2	64.0	60.9	64.9
Minimum	1.7	2.1	1.5	1.7
Coefficient of variation	0.56	0.53	0.53	0.54
DISTSH[f] (percentages)				
Mean	9.1	9.8	9.1	8.8
Standard deviation	3.6	3.7	3.2	3.0
Maximum	20.9	25.2	20.5	20.7
Minimum	2.2	2.1	2.0	2.0
Coefficient of variation	0.40	0.38	0.36	0.34
PSFINSH[g] (percentages)				
Mean	4.5	4.8	5.1	5.9
Standard deviation	2.1	2.2	2.5	2.8
Maximum	18.3	19.2	24.0	27.6
Minimum	1.8	1.8	1.5	1.8
Coefficient of variation	0.47	0.46	0.48	0.48
PSOTHSH[h] (percentages)				
Mean	4.9	6.6	8.9	9.9
Standard deviation	2.6	2.4	3.3	4.0
Maximum	27.1	17.9	21.1	31.7
Minimum	1.4	2.1	2.5	2.9
Coefficient of variation	0.52	0.37	0.37	0.40
ACSSH[i] (percentages)				
Mean	5.8	7.1	10.3	11.9
Standard deviation	2.1	2.2	3.0	3.4
Maximum	24.2	26.1	33.7	36.0
Minimum	1.4	1.6	3.0	3.9
Coefficient of variation	0.36	0.31	0.29	0.29

Table 4.1. (*Continued*)

Variable	1969	1979	1989	1996
GPDISSH[i] (percentages)				
Mean	39.6	38.8	33.4	30.8
Standard deviation	14.3	13.1	11.1	10.5
Maximum	66.4	67.6	66.4	68.0
Minimum	4.3	4.8	5.5	4.5
Coefficient of variation	0.36	0.34	0.33	0.34
INFOSH[k] (percentages)				
Mean	15.3	18.5	24.2	27.8
Standard deviation	4.7	4.9	5.9	6.6
Maximum	38.6	38.2	40.7	48.5
Minimum	4.8	5.5	6.9	8.7
Coefficient of variation	30.7	26.3	24.3	23.8

	1969–1996	1969–1979	1979–1996
PCTCHPCPI[l] (percentages)			
Mean	50.8	24.2	21.7
Standard deviation	15.5	9.6	11.9
Maximum	99.5	66.6	55.6
Minimum	12.5	3.4	−12.5
Coefficient of variation	0.31	0.40	0.55
PCTCHPOP[m] (percentages)			
Mean	49.7	19.1	22.2
Standard deviation	60.3	19.1	25.5
Maximum	432.6	131.0	138.9
Minimum	−16.4	−6.0	−16.8
Coefficient of variation	1.21	1.00	1.15
PCTCHEMP[n] (percentages)			
Mean	59.9	28.0	32.0
Standard deviation	33.3	16.9	19.0
Maximum	184.6	90.6	95.8
Minimum	−9.2	−10.0	−16.3
Coefficient of variation	0.56	0.60	0.59

Sources: BEA 1998a, and U.S. Census Bureau decennial censuses, 1970, 1980, and 1990.

[a]PCPI = Per capita personal income in 1992 dollars.

[b]POP = Population in thousands.

[c]COLL = Percent of adults (age 25+) with at least college degrees. Values are for 1970, 1980, and 1990.

[d]PRMSH = Percent of metropolitan earnings in the primary production group.

[e]MFGSH = Percent of metropolitan earnings in the manufacturing group.

[f]DISTSH = Percent of metropolitan earnings in the distribution group.

[g]PSFINSH = Percent of metropolitan earnings in the financial producer services group.

[h]PSOTHSH = Percent of metropolitan earnings in the other producer services group.

[i]ACSSH = Percent of metropolitan earnings in the advanced consumer services group.

[j]GPDISSH = Percent of metropolitan earnings in the goods production and distribution sector, i.e., GPDISSH = PRMSH + MFGSH + DISTSH.

[k]INFOSH = Percent of metropolitan earnings in the information sector, i.e., INFOSH = PFINSH + PSOTHSH + ACSSH.

[l]PCTCHPCPI = Percent change in per capita personal income.

[m]PCTCHPOP = Percent change in population.

[n]PCTCHEMP = Percent change in employment.

only 0.08 in 1970 and 0.05 in 1990 (Drennan and Lobo 1997), compared with 0.35 and 0.31 for the college variable. Second, the occupational mix of three of the six traded goods and services groups have high proportions of managerial, professional, and technical jobs, jobs that very often require college or even higher education (see Table 1.1).

As noted in Chapter 3, the relative mix of traded goods and services sectors has changed markedly for U.S. metropolitan areas over the almost thirty years covered. The primary production group mean share (PRMSH) and the manufacturing group mean share (MFGSH) have both fallen, although the latter continues to be the largest traded goods and services group on average. Although its mean share has diminished, the variation in the manufacturing share among metropolitan areas continues to be substantial, as measured by the coefficient of variation. Indeed, the maximum share of manufacturing earnings is over 60% in each of the years. The maximum share for the other traded goods and services sectors never exceeds 36%. In 1969, the distribution group was the second largest of the six traded goods and services groups, based upon a mean share of earnings of 9%. It has continued at that level. The three remaining groups, all traded services rather than traded goods, show increases in their mean relative shares of metropolitan earnings. The financial producer services group (PSFIN) increased the least: from 4.5% to 5.9%. The mean share of the other producer services group (PSOTHSH) rose from 5% to 10%, and the mean share of the advanced consumer services group (ACSSH) went from 6% to 12%.

The percent change in real per capita personal income (PCTCHPCPI) averaged 51% over the full period, 1969 to 1996. The first 10 years, 1969 to 1979, had better growth, 24%, than the last 17 years, 22%. Not only was the growth weaker after 1979, it was also far more variable. The coefficient of variation, which was 0.40 in the 1969 to 1979 period, increased to 0.55 in the 1979 to 1996 period. The slowing of per capita personal income growth and the increased variability of that growth among metropolitan areas suggests that the two subperiods are dissimilar. On the other hand, mean population growth (PCTCHPOP) is similar in the two subperiods. Mean employment growth is much higher than mean population growth for every period, reflecting the fact that labor force participation has risen, primarily because of the increased participation by women. All of the means in Table 4.1 are simple means. Otherwise they would reflect characteristics of the very largest metropolitan areas.

Econometric Estimation Results

Specialization and Size

I have estimated equation (4.7), regressing the relative earnings share in each of six traded goods and services groups on population and population squared. The equation was estimated for 1969 and 1996. The results are shown in Table 4.2. As noted above, the hypothesis that relative earnings share increases with population up to some maximum infers that the coefficient on population is positive while the coefficient on the squared population is negative. Five of the twelve estimated equations are not shown because they did not have any statistically significant coefficients. Of the seven equations presented in Table 4.2, all have significant positive coefficients on the population term, and all have the expected negative coefficient on the population squared term, although they are not all significant. The final column of Table 4.2 shows the calculated population at which the relative earnings share is a maximum, calculated by setting the derivative, dSH/dPOP, equal to zero and then solving for population. For 1969, the estimated population at which the manufacturing share is a maximum is 9.5 million. For distribution it is 10.9 million. The two producer service groups attain their maximum shares at much higher populations: 20.7 million for finan-

Table 4.2. Regression Estimates: Specialization Shares Related to Population, 1969 and 1996

| Dependent Variables | Independent Variables (coefficients and absolute t statistics) | | R^2 | POP at Which Share Is Maximum (thousands) |
	POP	POP^2		
MFGSH69	2.45E-05 (2.0)	−1.29E-09 (1.6)	0.01	9,496
DISTSH69	1.02E-05 (3.4)	−4.68E-10 (2.3)	0.04	10,897
PSFINSH69	4.38E-06 (2.5)	−1.06E-10 (0.9)	0.04	20,660
PSOTHSH69	5.86E-06 (2.7)	−1.81E-10 (1.3)	0.04	16,188
DISTSH96	8.85E-06 (4.0)	−4.53E-10 (3.1)	0.05	9,768
PSFINSH96	9.70E-06 (4.9)	−2.69E-10 (2.1)	0.16	18,030
PSOTHSH96	2.57E-05 (10.5)	−1.15E-09 (7.2)	0.33	11,174

Source: Calculated for this study from BEA 1998a.

cial producer services (PSFINSH69) and 16.2 million for other producer services (PSOTHSH69).

The estimated equation for the manufacturing share in 1996 is not shown, because it has no significant coefficients. The inference is that the positive relationship between the relative share of earnings from manufacturing and population size that is evident for 1969 was no longer present in 1996. The relationship between the distribution share and population in the 1996 equation is quite similar to that in the 1969 equation, and the estimated population at which the distribution share is a maximum is roughly similar in both years (10.9 and 9.8 million, respectively).

Unlike the distribution share equations, the two producer service equations for 1996 exhibit interesting differences compared with their 1969 equations. Although the estimated population at which the financial producer services share reaches a maximum is 2.5 million lower in the 1996 equation, both numbers approximate the population of the largest metropolitan area, the New York CMSA. The adjusted R^2 of the 1996 equation for financial producer services is 0.16 compared with only 0.04 in the 1969 equation, and the squared term is statistically significant in the 1996 equation but is not in the 1969 equation. The other producer services equation for 1996 has an estimated population, at which the share is a maximum, of 11.2 million, 5.0 million lower than the 1969 equation. Also, the adjusted R^2 jumps up to 0.33 in the 1996 equation, compared with only 0.04 in the 1969 equation; and the squared term is highly significant, unlike the 1969 equation.

A number of inferences follow from those results. The weak relationship between the relative share of manufacturing earnings and population in 1969 is totally absent in 1996. The relationship between the relative share of distribution earnings and population in 1969 is pretty much unchanged in 1996. The two producer service groups, however, apparently have a much stronger relationship between relative share and population size in 1996 than in 1969. The answer to the fourth question posed at the beginning of this chapter, Is specialization positively related to metropolitan size?, depends upon the specialization. For the primary group and the advanced consumer services group, neither of which has significant equations, the answer is no. For the manufacturing group, the answer is not any longer. For the distribution group, the answer is yes. For the two producer services groups, the answer is yes, and the relationship has become stronger over time.

Level of Real per Capita Personal Income

The estimation of equation (4.6) tests the effects of specialization, human capital, and size upon the level of metropolitan income. However, equation (4.6) presents two estimation problems. The first is an endogeneity problem with the equation as specified because the college variable may be an effect of high income as well as a cause of high income. Cheshire and Mills (1999) have argued that there is always a problem using some educational attainment measure as an explanatory variable. "If education contributed nothing to productivity, a rich country would nevertheless provide lots of it for its children because people believe it contributes to the quality of life. . . . Undoubtedly, the truth is that education is both a cause and an effect of prosperity" (Cheshire and Mills 1999, p. 1332). To avoid the endogeneity problem, having a dependent variable on the right-hand side of the equation, I estimated a two-equation model by means of two-stage least squares. The first equation is equation (4.6), in which the variable COLL was estimated from the set of appropriate instruments. In the second equation, COLL is regressed upon COLL lagged ten years, the log of population, and most importantly, the log of per capita personal income. The two-equation model deals with the simultaneity issue Cheshire and Mills (1999) raised.

However, the second estimation problem with equation (4.6) is that the measure of specialization in other producer services (PSOTHSH) is highly correlated with the college attainment variable (the simple correlation between them in 1996 is +0.50, as shown in Table 4.4). In estimations that included both COLL and PSOTHSH, the latter had a negative, insignificant coefficient. In estimations that excluded COLL, the coefficient on PSOTHSH was positive and significant. Consequently, I have dropped the two-stage least squares model. Instead I have estimated equation (4.6) by ordinary least squares without the college attainment variable. It is also estimated without the measure of specialization for the primary production group (PRMSH), because that variable, although positive and significant for the first subperiod, 1969–79, is not significant in any of the other periods.

Table 4.3. Regression Estimates: Logarithm of per Capita Personal Income, 1969, 1979, 1989, and 1996

	LPCPI69	LPCPI79	LPCPI89	LPCPI96
Intercept	9.0836	9.4086	9.3041	9.3774
	(207.0)	(157.2)	(171.4)	(176.4)
LPOP	0.0565	−0.0080	0.0289	0.0160
	(8.0)	(1.2)	(3.1)	(1.8)
MFGSH	0.1362	0.3188	0.3749	0.4598
	(2.41)	(4.9)	(4.8)	(5.9)
DISTSH	−0.6599	0.3514	−0.6049	−0.0408
	(3.2)	(1.8)	(2.5)	(0.2)
PSFINSH	2.2741	1.7778	2.1847	2.2538
	(6.2)	(4.9)	(6.0)	(7.8)
PSOTHSH	1.1220	2.9023	1.9356	1.6069
	(3.8)	(8.2)	(5.9)	(6.4)
ACSSH	0.3593	−0.0083	0.6942	0.5258
	(1.0)	(0.0)	(2.8)	(2.6)
SOUTH	−0.1545	−0.1351	−0.0853	−0.0572
	(10.5)	(9.1)	(5.7)	(4.0)
adj. R^2	0.56	0.48	0.52	0.52
F statistic	50.5	36.0	42.0	42.7
n	269	269	269	269

Source: Calculated for this study from BEA 1998a.
  Note: Absolute values of t statistics in parentheses.

The estimated ordinary least squares equation results for 1969, 1979, 1989, and 1996 are in Table 4.3. The adjusted R^2 ranges from 0.56 for the 1969 equation to 0.48 for the 1979 equation. The effect of population on the level of metropolitan per capita income is ambiguous. In the 1969 equation, the coefficient on the log of population variable (LPOP) is positive and highly significant. However, in the 1979 equation, it is near zero and insignificant. It is positive and significant in the 1989 equation, but only half as large as in the 1969 equation. Finally, the LPOP coefficient in the 1996 equation is near zero and not quite significant. If those varying results are summarized, one may note that the positive effect of population size upon the level of metropolitan per capita income has diminished over the past few decades.

There is very little ambiguity about the effect of specialization upon the level of metropolitan income. For most of the specializations and for most of the years, the effect of specialization upon the level of metropolitan per capita income is positive and significant. Recall that the specialization measure for the primary production group has been excluded because it is insignificant for most of the years. The coefficient on the measure of specialization for manufacturing

(MFGSH) group is positive and significant in all four years, and the size of the coefficient increases in each year after 1969. Thus, specialization in manufacturing appears to raise the level of metropolitan per capita income in all four years.

That is not the case for specialization in the other group of the goods production and distribution sector, namely distribution. In both the 1969 and the 1989 equations, the coefficient on the relative share of metropolitan earnings from the distribution group (DISTSH) is negative and significant. It is positive in only one equation, 1979, but it is not quite significant. In the 1996 equation, the coefficient on the distribution share variable is near zero and insignificant. Specialization in the distribution group appears to lower the level of metropolitan per capita income, or to have no effect.

The coefficients on the measures of specialization in each of the two producer services groups are always positive, significant, and larger than any of the other coefficients on specialization variables. Thus, specialization in either producer service group raises the level of metropolitan income. For the third of the information sector groups, the effect of specialization in advanced consumer services upon the level of metropolitan per capita income is nonexistent in the equations for the earlier years, 1969 and 1979. However, in the 1989 and 1996 equations, the coefficient on the advanced consumer services share variable (ACSSH) is positive and significant.

I included a regional dummy variable (SOUTH) to capture regional differences in per capita income. Two other regional dummy variables were tested, for the west and midwest, but they were never significant. The coefficient on SOUTH is negative and significant in all four equations, indicating that metropolitan areas in the south tend to have lower levels of per capita income. However, the coefficient on SOUTH is smaller by almost half in the 1989 and 1996 equations compared with the 1969 and 1979 equations, indicating a reduction in the adverse effect upon per capita income of location in the south.

The simple correlations among all of the variables used (and some not used) in the equations described above are shown in Table 4.4. The top matrix shows the 1969 variables, and the bottom matrix the 1996 variables. Note that the only specialization measure that has a negative correlation with the log of per capita personal income (LPCPI) is the share of earnings in the primary production group (PRMSH), and that is true for both years. As noted above, the college at-

Table 4.4. Simple Correlation Matrix, 1969 and 1996 Variables

	ACSSH69	COLL70	DISTSH69	LPCPI69	LPOP69	MFGSH69	PRMSH69	PSFINSH69	PSOTHSH69
ACSSH69	1.00	0.10	0.17	0.22	0.01	−0.07	−0.05	0.26	0.13
COLL70	0.10	1.00	−0.17	0.16	0.02	−0.41	−0.04	0.23	0.30
DISTSH69	0.17	−0.17	1.00	0.07	0.30	−0.08	0.00	0.28	0.11
LPCPI69	0.22	0.16	0.07	1.00	0.51	0.17	−0.17	0.31	0.27
LPOP69	0.01	0.02	0.30	0.51	1.00	0.21	−0.33	0.20	0.21
MFGSH69	−0.07	−0.41	−0.08	0.17	0.21	1.00	−0.39	−0.28	−0.31
PRMSH69	−0.05	−0.04	0.00	−0.17	−0.33	−0.39	1.00	−0.05	−0.02
PSFINSH69	0.26	0.23	0.28	0.31	0.20	−0.28	−0.05	1.00	0.25
PSOTHSH69	0.13	0.30	0.11	0.27	0.21	−0.31	−0.02	0.25	1.00

	ACSSH96	COLL90	DISTSH96	LPCPI96	LPOP96	MFGSH96	PRMSH96	PSFINSH96	PSOTHSH96
ACSSH96	1.00	−0.10	0.08	0.04	−0.13	−0.14	−0.18	0.03	−0.07
COLL90	−0.10	1.00	−0.14	0.47	0.25	−0.30	−0.20	0.36	0.50
DISTSH96	0.08	−0.14	1.00	0.16	0.26	−0.07	0.03	0.24	0.13
LPCPI96	0.04	0.47	0.16	1.00	0.51	0.04	−0.23	0.55	0.51
LPOP96	−0.13	0.25	0.26	0.51	1.00	−0.07	0.04	0.46	0.64
MFGSH96	−0.14	−0.30	−0.07	0.04	−0.07	1.00	−0.28	−0.29	−0.37
PRMSH96	−0.18	−0.20	0.03	−0.23	−0.16	−0.28	1.00	−0.19	−0.13
PSFINSH96	0.03	0.36	0.24	0.55	0.46	−0.29	−0.19	1.00	0.43
PSOTHSH96	−0.07	0.50	0.13	0.51	0.64	−0.37	−0.13	0.43	1.00

Source: Calculated for this study from BEA 1998a.

tainment variable was excluded from the equations of Table 4.3 because its inclusion always changed the sign of the other producer services share coefficient from positive to negative and reduced its statistical significance. The reason for that effect is brought out in Table 4.4. The simple correlation between COLL and PSOTHSH is always higher than the simple correlation between COLL and the dependent variable, the log of per capita personal income. Both correlations are positive. That is not the case for COLL with the specialization measures for the three goods production and distribution groups: primary production (PRMSH), manufacturing (MFGSH), and distribution (DISTSH). All are negative in both years. That result is not surprising, given the nature of those activities. What is somewhat surprising is that the simple correlation between COLL and the measure of specialization in advanced consumer services is so low in 1969 ($+0.10$) and not only low but negative in 1996 (-0.10).

Perhaps the most interesting facts that emerge from Table 4.4 are the marked increases in the correlations among the level of per capita income and the two producer service groups (PSFINSH and PSOTHSH). For 1969 they are 0.31 and 0.27, respectively. For 1996 they are 0.55 and 0.51. The same pattern occurs with the measure of metropolitan size (LPOP) and the two producer service groups. For 1969 those correlations are 0.20 with PSFINSH and 0.21 with PSOTHSH. In 1996, however, they are 0.46 and 0.64. In the case of manufacturing, the change is in the opposite direction. For 1969, the correlations among the manufacturing share and income (LPCPI) and size (LPOP) are 0.17 and 0.21, respectively, while for 1996 they are 0.04 and -0.07.

Growth in per Capita Income, Population, and Employment

Estimated equations for growth of per capita income are shown in Table 4.5. Three equations are shown, one for each time period: 1969–96, 1969–79, and 1979–96. As noted above in discussing the descriptive statistics, the earliest period, 1969–79, appears to be quite different from the latest period, 1979–96. Therefore, I have estimated growth equations for those two subperiods, as well as for the long period, 1969–96. Because of the high correlation between the college attainment variable and the measure of specialization in other producer services noted above, I have aggregated the six specialization variables into two broad specialization variables. One measures specialization in all three goods production and distribution groups combined (GPDISSH). It is the sum of the

Table 4.5. Regression Estimates: Logarithm of Growth in per Capita Personal
Income, 1969 to 1996, 1969 to 1979, and 1979 to 1996

Variables at Beginning of Period	LDPCPI6996	LDPCPI6979	LDPCPI7996
Intercept	2.4674	2.1890	2.6840
	(6.8)	(7.2)	(7.0)
LPCPI	−0.2519	−0.2162	−0.3013
	(6.4)	(6.6)	(7.3)
COLL	0.0100	0	0.0082
	(6.6)	0.0	(7.3)
GPDISSH	0.2603	0.0116	0.3527
	(6.0)	(0.3)	(7.5)
INFOSH	0.5992	0.4630	0.7979
	(4.8)	(4.4)	(6.3)
SOUTH	0.0758	−0.0018	0.0531
	(6.2)	(0.2)	(4.5)
adj. R^2	0.38	0.18	0.34
F statistic	33.5	12.8	29
n	269	269	269

Source: Calculated for this study from BEA 1998a.
Note: Absolute values of t statistics in parentheses.

shares of metropolitan earnings in the primary production, manufacturing, and distribution groups. The other measures specialization in the three information groups combined (INFOSH); it is the sum of the earnings shares in the two producer service groups plus the advanced consumer services group. That aggregation enables me to estimate growth equations that include both measures of specialization and the level of college attainment.

In the three income growth equations, the dependent variable is the log difference of per capita income (LDPCPI) over the designated period, which is equivalent to the percentage change in per capita income. The right-hand variables include the level of metropolitan per capita income at the beginning of the period (LPCPI), college attainment of the adult population at the beginning of the period (COLL), the broad measures of specialization in the goods production and distribution sector (GPDISSH) and in the information sector (INFOSH) at the beginning of the period, and the regional dummy variable (SOUTH).

The first equation in Table 4.5 is for the long period, 1969–96, and there are no surprises. The coefficient on LPCPI is negative and significant, indicating that places with higher levels of initial income tend to have slower growth in per capita income. The coefficient on COLL is positive and significant, indicating that places with higher levels of college attainment in the initial year of the growth period have faster growth in per capita income. Location in a southern state also enhances growth of per capita income. The coefficient on the share of earnings in the goods production and distribution sector is positive and significant, as is the coefficient on the share of earnings from the information sector. Thus, each of the broad specializations contributes to the growth of per capita income. The adjusted R^2 is 0.38.

The equation for the first subperiod, 1969–79 is not nearly as good. The coefficient on the college variable drops to zero and is insignificant. The same is true for the coefficient on the share of earnings from goods production and distribution, and for the coefficient on the regional dummy variable. Only the information share variable continues to have a positive, significant coefficient. The adjusted R^2 is much lower: 0.18. Thus, the growth of per capita income of metropolitan areas over the ten years from 1969 to 1979 is not captured by those variables.

The estimated equations for the two subperiods are strikingly different from each other, suggesting that the underlying structure influencing per capita income growth is not the same in the two periods. The two periods differ a good deal in growth and in variability. Average growth of per capita income was 24.2% in the 1969–79 period and 21.7% in the 1979–96 period, despite its being a much longer period. Also, the coefficient of variation increased: from 0.40 in the 1969–79 period to 0.55 in the 1979–96 period (see Table 4.1). Thus, the equation for the full period, 1969–96, disguises or glosses over structural shifts. The equation for the second subperiod, 1979–96, is much like the equation for the full period. All of the coefficients are significant, and all have the expected signs. The adjusted R^2 is 0.34, similar to the first equation. Thus, specialization in either sector, higher college attainment, and location in the south are all initial conditions that enhance growth of per capita income from 1979 to 1996. Higher initial per capita income depresses per capita income growth.

Estimated equations for the log difference of population growth for the long period and for the two subperiods are presented in Table 4.6. Unlike the per capita income growth equations, the college variable was never significant and so it is not included. The exclusion of the college variable made it possible to use the six individual specialization groups rather than just the two broad sectors of specialization, goods production and distribution, and information. Included on the right-hand side, in addition to the initial values of the six specialization groups, are initial size (LPOP) and the regional dummy variable (SOUTH).

Table 4.6. Regression Estimates: Logarithm of Growth in Population,
1969 to 1996, 1969 to 1979, and 1979 to 1996

Variables at Beginning of Period	LDPOP6996	LDPOP6979	LDPOP7996
Intercept	0.4402	0.2613	0.2507
	(4.1)	(5.4)	(3.4)
LPOP	−0.0130	−0.0212	0.0093
	(0.8)	(3.1)	(0.9)
PRMSH	0.8391	0.3593	0.1212
	(2.8)	(2.6)	(0.6)
MFGSH	−0.8991	−0.3523	−0.6424
	(7.0)	(6.1)	(6.6)
DISTSH	−2.0724	−0.7976	−1.4146
	(4.8)	(4.1)	(5.4)
PSFINSH	3.9756	1.8813	1.2729
	(5.2)	(5.4)	(2.6)
PSOTHSH	1.9426	0.7833	1.0436
	(3.2)	(2.8)	(2.1)
ACSSH	0.5893	0.3171	0.2950
	(0.8)	(1.0)	(0.7)
SOUTH	0.0869	0.0439	0.0410
	(2.8)	(3.2)	(2.1)
adj. R^2	0.48	0.47	0.39
F statistic	31.5	30.8	22.8
n	269	269	269
	LDPOP6996	LDPOP6979	LDPOP7996
Intercept	0.5347	0.3020	0.3115
	(5.9)	(7.4)	(4.0)
LPOP	−0.0202	−0.0240	−0.0055
	(1.4)	(3.7)	(0.7)
GPDISSH	−1.1272	−0.4447	−0.7337
	(9.7)	(8.5)	(9.5)
INFOSH	1.7677	0.8285	0.7248
	(5.2)	(5.4)	(3.6)
SOUTH	0.0893	0.0456	0.0421
	(2.9)	(3.3)	(2.2)
adj. R^2	0.45	0.44	0.38
F statistic	54.9	54.2	42.2
n	269	269	269

Source: Calculated for this study from BEA 1998a.
  Note: Absolute values of t statistics in parentheses.

Coefficients on the manufacturing and distribution shares are negative and significant in all three of the population growth equations. Coefficients on the financial and other producer services shares are positive and significant in all three equations. The advanced consumer services share always has a positive coefficient, but it is never significant. Specialization in the primary production group also raises population growth, but in the latest period, 1979 to 1996, its coefficient is close to zero and is not significant. The regional dummy variable is always positive and significant. The coefficient on the log of initial population is close to zero and insignificant in all but the 1969–79 equation. The adjusted R^2 values are higher than for the per capita income growth equations, ranging from 0.39 to 0.48.

I also estimated population growth equations for the same three periods, using the aggregated measures of specialization rather than the six individual specialization measures. Those equations are also shown in Table 4.6. The coefficient on the initial goods production and distribution share (GPDISSH) is negative and significant in all three periods. The coefficient on the initial information share (INFOSH) is positive and significant in all three periods.

The key findings from the population growth equations are that specialization in manufacturing or distribution reduces metropolitan population growth while specialization in financial or other producer services increases metropolitan population growth. Specialization in advanced consumer services has no significant effect upon population growth, while specialization in the primary production group enhances population growth in the earlier subperiod but has no effect in the later subperiod. When the specializations are aggregated, goods production and distribution specialization always reduces population growth, while information sector specialization always enhances growth.

Last of all, I present the interesting employment growth equations. The employment measure used is from the BEA Regional Economic Information System. It is the most comprehensive employment data available for metropolitan areas. It includes all full-time and part-time workers, as does the BLS series of nonagricultural employment, but it additionally includes all the self-employed as well as agricultural workers. Estimated equations for the log difference of metropolitan employment for the long period, 1969–96, and for the two subperiods, 1969–79 and 1979–96, are shown in Table 4.7. The form of the equations is the same as for the population growth equations except that initial employment in log form replaces the log of initial population. And as with the population equations, the college variable is not included in the equations that include the six initial specialization variables, because of its high correlation with the share of earnings in other producer services (PSOTHSH).

The equation for the long period has negative, significant coefficients on both the manufacturing share and on the distribution share, while it has positive, sig-

Table 4.7. Regression Estimates: Logarithm of Growth in Employment, 1969 to 1996, 1969 to 1979, and 1979 to 1996

Variables at Beginning of Period	LDEMP6996	LDEMP6979	LDEMP7996
Intercept	0.9458	0.4628	0.4892
	(4.9)	(5.0)	(4.1)
LEMP	−0.0387	−0.0314	−0.0013
	(2.4)	(4.0)	(0.1)
PRMSH	0.4131	0.6739	−0.6265
	(1.2)	(4.2)	(3.1)
MFGSH	−0.8817	−0.3267	−0.6843
	(6.4)	(4.9)	(6.8)
DISTSH	−1.2218	−0.1630	−1.2088
	(2.6)	(0.7)	(4.5)
PSFINSH	4.5662	2.2372	1.4148
	(5.5)	(5.6)	(2.7)
PSOTHSH	2.2738	1.4948	0.7148
	(3.4)	(4.7)	(1.4)
ACSSH	1.3661	1.0917	0.4403
	(1.7)	(2.9)	(0.9)
SOUTH	0.0392	0.0116	0.0299
	(1.2)	(0.7)	(1.5)
adj. R^2	0.46	0.49	0.35
F statistic	27.3	33.6	19.2
n	269	269	269
	LDEMP6996	LDEMP6979	LDEMP7996
Intercept	0.5736	0.4506	0.0355
	(2.8)	(4.4)	(0.3)
LEMP	−0.0471	−0.0384	−0.0054
	(3.2)	(5.1)	(0.5)
LCOLL	0.1896	0.0690	0.1241
	(3.2)	(2.3)	(3.2)
GPDISSH	−0.7693	−0.3472	−0.4902
	(5.5)	(5.0)	(5.2)
INFOSH	2.3221	1.4535	0.8002
	(6.5)	(8.1)	(3.4)
SOUTH	0.0791	0.0211	0.0587
	(2.4)	(1.3)	(2.9)
adj. R^2	0.45	0.46	0.34
F statistic	44.8	47.0	28.8
n	269	269	269

Source: Calculated for this study from BEA 1998a.
Note: Absolute values of t statistics in parentheses.

nificant coefficients on the two producer services shares. The other two specialization shares, primary production and advanced consumer services, are positive but insignificant. Thus, initial specialization in the two large goods production and distribution groups reduces subsequent employment growth, while initial specialization in the two producer services groups contributes to employment growth. Initial metropolitan total employment has a negative significant coefficient, indicating that large places tend to have slower employment growth. The regional dummy variable has a positive but insignificant coefficient, and that is the case for the subperiod equations as well. The adjusted R^2 is 0.46, which is about the same as for the population growth equation for the long period.

The equation for the first subperiod, 1969–79 contains few surprises. The manufacturing and distribution share coefficients continue to be negative, although the distribution share coefficient is insignificant. The two producer service shares continue to have positive and significant coefficients. Reflecting the run-up in energy prices in the 1970s, the coefficient on the primary production share is positive and highly significant. The advanced consumer services share also has a positive, significant coefficient. The coefficient on the log of initial total employment continues negative and significant. The adjusted R^2 is a bit higher: 0.49.

In the equation for the more recent subperiod, 1979–96, all three of the goods production and distribution initial shares have negative, significant coefficients. All three of the information sector initial shares have positive coefficients, but only one of them, PSFINSH, is significant. Interestingly, the coefficient on the log of initial employment falls to zero and insignificance, suggesting that the size of the metropolitan area did not affect employment growth in that most recent period.

In order to include the initial value of the college attainment variable, I also estimated employment growth equations for the same three periods, using the aggregated measures of specialization rather than the six individual specialization shares. They are also shown in Table 4.7. Note that the effect of the college variable on employment growth is always positive and significant. The effect of the initial share of the goods production and distribution sector is negative and significant in all equations, while the effect of the information sector is always positive and significant. As with the first set of employment growth equations, the effect of initial total employment is negative and significant except in the last equation, 1979–96, where it is around zero and insignificant. The regional dummy is always positive and it is significant in all but one of the three periods, 1969–79. The adjusted R^2 values are similar to those in the first set of equations in Table 4.7.

Table 4.8. Effect of One Standard
Deviation Increase in Variable Named
upon per Capita Income, 1969 and 1996
(percentages)

Variable	1969[a]	1996[b]
LPOP	1.8	6.5
MFGSH	4.8	1.9
DISTSH	−0.1	−2.3
PSFINSH	6.6	4.9
PSOTHSH	6.6	2.9
ACSSH	1.8	0.8
SOUTH[c]	−3.2	−8.3

Source: Calculated using equations in Table 4.3
and data in Table 4.1.
[a]Mean per capita income was $13,254.
[b]Mean per capita income was $19,869.
[c]Effect on per capita income of location in the
south.

Discussion and Conclusion

I have used the estimated equations in Table 4.3 for the first year, 1969, and
the last year, 1996, to calculate the separate effect upon real per capita income
of a one standard deviation rise from the mean in each one of the variables. Those
calculations are summarized in Table 4.8. Raising the log of population (size)
one standard deviation boosts real per capita income by 1.8% in 1969 and 6.5%
in 1996. Location in the south always lowers per capita income, but curiously
the size of the reduction increases from −3.2% in 1969 to −8.3% in 1996. A
one standard deviation rise in the manufacturing share raises per capita income
by 4.8% in 1969, but only 1.9% in 1996. For the distribution sector, the effect
is negative in both years. A one standard deviation rise above the mean in the
share of the financial producer services sector raises the level of per capita income 6.6% in 1969 and 4.9% in 1996. A one standard deviation rise in the share
of other producer services has a large positive effect in 1969, 6.6%, but a smaller
effect in 1996, 2.9%. Advanced consumer services has a small positive effect in
both years.

Thus, specialization and size raise the level of per capita income, except in the
distribution group. The magnitude of the effects differ from 1969 to 1996. In the
earlier year, specialization in either of the two producer service groups adds more

to the level of income than any other variable (6.6% for each), followed by specialization in manufacturing, which adds 4.8%. Specialization in advanced consumer services and metropolitan size each add less than 2% to the level of income in 1969. However, in 1996, size adds more to the level of income than any other variable (6.5%). The two producer service groups add about 5% (finance) and 3% (other). Specialization in manufacturing adds 2% to the level of income.

I have used the three per capita income growth equations (Table 4.5) to calculate the effects on growth rates of raising the value of each independent variable one standard deviation above its mean. The results are shown in Table 4.9. Raising initial per capita income (LPCPI) of a metropolitan area one standard deviation above average metropolitan per capita income in 1969 reduces the income growth by 6.9 percentage points over the 1969–96 period. That is a rather large effect, considering that average per capita real income increased 51% from 1969 to 1996. For the first subperiod, 1969–79, the reduction in growth is slightly less, −4.8 percentage points, while for the second subperiod, 1979–96, the effect is similar to the long period, namely a drop of −6.3 percentage points. College attainment one standard deviation above the 1969 mean adds 5.3 percentage points to per capita income growth from 1969 to 1996. It adds nothing in the 1969–79 period (−0.4 percentage points) but adds 4.6 percentage points in the more recent period. The effect of boosting the share of earnings in goods production and distribution (GPDISSH) by one standard deviation raises per capita income growth 5.0 percentage points in the 1969 to 1996 period and about the same in the 1979 to 1996 period. As with the college variable, the initial value of GPDISSH adds nothing to per capita income growth in the 1969–79 period. The initial value of specialization in the information sector (INFOSH)

Table 4.9. Effect of One Standard Deviation Increase in Variable Named upon Growth in per Capita Income
(percentages)

	1969–1996	1969–1979	1979–1996
Average growth	50.8	24.2	21.7
LPCPI	−6.9	−4.8	−6.3
COLL	5.3	−0.4	4.6
GPDISSH	5.0	−0.2	5.1
INFOSH	3.6	2.3	4.2
SOUTH	5.8	−0.5	3.0

Source: Calculated using equations in Table 4.5 and data in Table 4.1.

Table 4.10. Effect of One Standard Deviation Increase in Variable Named
upon Growth in Population
(percentages)

	1969–1996	1969–1996	1969–1979	1979–1996
Average growth	49.7	49.7	19.1	22.2
LPOP	−1.7	−3.1	−3.1	−0.7
GPDISSH	—	−21.0	−7.2	−11.0
INFOSH	—	12.2	4.7	4.3
SOUTH	4.9	7.2	3.0	2.9
PRMSH	4.5	—	—	—
MFGSH	−12.7	—	—	—
DISTSH	−7.4	—	—	—
PSFINSH	8.4	—	—	—
PSOTHSH	5.0	—	—	—
ACSSH	1.2	—	—	—

Source: Calculated using equations in Table 4.6 and data in Table 4.1.

adds to the growth of per capita income in all three periods. The amount added is slightly smaller than the amount added by a one standard deviation rise in GPDISSH in both the 1969–96 period and in the 1979–96 period. Location in the south adds 5.8 percentage points to per capita income growth in the 1969–96 period.

I have similarly used four of the population growth equations (Table 4.6) to calculate the effects on growth rates of raising the value of each independent variable one standard deviation above its mean. The results are shown in Table 4.10. For the long period in which the six individual measures of group specialization are included, 1969–96, growth in metropolitan population is most adversely affected by initial specialization in manufacturing and distribution. Population growth is most positively affected by specialization in financial and other producer services. The effects are not trivial. Raising the manufacturing share in 1969 by one standard deviation reduces the 1969–96 population growth by 12.7 percentage points. Note that the average metropolitan population growth over that period is 49.7%. Raising the distribution share by one standard deviation cuts population growth by 7.4 percentage points. One of the three goods production and distribution groups, primary production, shows a positive effect on population growth, raising it 4.5 percentage points. But bigger positive effects come from financial and other producer services. Raising the financial producer services share by one standard deviation increases population growth by 8.4 percentage points, and in the case of other producer services the addition to population growth is 5.0 percentage points. A slight positive effect is added by advanced consumer services (1.2 percentage points) and a slight negative effect by the log of population (-1.7 percentage points). Location in the south adds 4.9 percentage points to population growth.

The three equations that use the aggregated specialization shares show more dramatic effects upon population growth. A one standard deviation increase in the share of specialization in the goods production and distribution sector reduces population growth -21.0 percentage points in the long period, 1969–96, -7.2 percentage points in the 1969–79 period, and -11.0 percentage points in the 1979–96 period. On the other hand, a one standard deviation increase in the share of specialization in the information sector increases population growth 12.2 percentage points in the long period, 1969–96, 4.7 percentage points in the 1969–79 period, and 4.3 percentage points in the 1979–96 period. Raising initial population by one standard deviation lowers population growth 3.1 percentage points in both the 1969–96 and 1969–79 periods, and much less, -0.7 percentage points, in the 1979–96 period. Location in the south raises population growth 7.2 percentage points, 1969–96, and about 3 percentage points in each of the two subperiods.

Finally, I have used some of the employment growth equations (Table 4.7) to calculate the effects on growth of increasing the value of each independent variable one standard deviation above its mean. Those results are in Table 4.11. The first calculation uses the long period equation in which all six measures of group

Table 4.11. Effect of One Standard Deviation Increase in Variable Named upon Growth in Employment
(percentages)

	1969–1996	1969–1996	1969–1979	1979–1996
Average growth	59.9	59.9	28.0	32.0
LEMP	−5.1	−6.2	−5.1	−0.7
LCOLL	—	6.0	2.2	3.7
GPDISSH	—	−11.0	−5.0	−6.4
INFOSH	—	10.9	6.8	3.9
SOUTH	2.2	4.4	1.2	3.3
PRMSH	2.2	—	—	—
MFGSH	−12.4	—	—	—
DISTSH	−4.4	—	—	—
PSFINSH	9.7	—	—	—
PSOTHSH	5.8	—	—	—
ACSSH	2.9	—	—	—

Source: Calculated using equations in Table 4.6 and data in Table 4.1.

specialization are included. The results are similar to the effects on population growth, which is not surprising, given the length of the period: 27 years. The largest negative effect on employment growth, −12.4 percentage points, is from raising the initial share of earnings in manufacturing by one standard deviation. Employment growth over the period averaged 59.9%. Raising the distribution share by one standard deviation reduces employment growth −4.4 percentage points. The largest positive effects on employment growth are from raising the initial share of earnings in financial producer services by one standard deviation (9.7 percentage points) and doing the same to other producer services (5.8 percentage points). Increasing by one standard deviation the shares of both the primary production group and the advanced consumer services group has smaller positive effects on employment growth. Raising initial total employment by one standard deviation cuts employment growth by −5.1 percentage points. Location in the south raises employment growth 2.2 percentage points.

The three employment growth equations that use the aggregated shares, goods production and distribution and information, include the college attainment variable. Raising the initial college variable by one standard deviation above its mean adds 6.0 percentage points to employment growth in the 1969–96 period and smaller amounts in the two subperiods, as one would expect, because the percent employment growth for the two subperiods sum to the full period growth. Boosting the goods production and distribution share one standard deviation cuts growth in employment −11.0 percentage points in the full period and by smaller negative amounts in the subperiods. Doing the same to the information share, however, increases growth in employment by +10.9 percentage points for the 1969–96 period, with smaller positive effects in the subperiods. Initial employment raised one standard deviation lowers employment growth −6.2 percentage points in the long period, −5.1 percentage points in the 1969–79 period, and has almost no effect in the 1979–96 period. Location in the south raises employment growth 4.4 percentage points, 1969–96 and smaller positive amounts in the subperiods.

These results, showing a large, positive effect of human capital upon metropolitan employment growth combined with a large, negative effect of the initial share of the economy in goods production and distribution, are corroborated by a recent econometric analysis for a longer period (Simon 1998). In that paper, metropolitan employment growth for decades, beginning 1940–50 and ending

1980–86, is regressed upon initial share of manufacturing employment in the metropolitan area, initial human capital, regional dummy variables, and other controls. The human capital is measured by high school graduates for all decades and college graduates for the most recent decades. The human capital variables have a positive, significant effect upon employment growth in all decades. Interestingly, the manufacturing share variable has a negative coefficient in each of the three decades from 1960 forward and a positive coefficient in the two earlier decades. The author, who is not seeking to measure the effects of specialization, does not remark about that shift. Those results do support my view that the contribution of a specialization to metropolitan growth can change from positive to negative, or the reverse, depending upon the relative growth in national demand.

The seven questions posed at the beginning of this chapter can be answered in light of the above analysis.

1. Does specialization improve the level of income more than diversity? Specialization generally improves the level of income in the four years tested, although specialization in distribution reduces the level of income (see Table 4.3).

2. Do some specializations add more to the level of income than others? Specialization in either of the two producer service groups adds more to the level of metropolitan income than specialization in manufacturing. Specialization in advanced consumer services adds very little to the level of income, much less than is added by specialization in manufacturing (see Table 4.8).

3. Is the effect of specialization upon the level of income different in different time periods? Yes. The four specializations with positive effects upon the level of income all have larger effects in the first year (1969) than in the last year (1996). Specialization in distribution, however, has a larger negative effect in the last year (see Table 4.8).

4. Is specialization positively related to metropolitan size? For three groups, distribution, financial producer services, and other producer services, the share of earnings rises with metropolitan size in both 1969 and 1996. That is also the case for the manufacturing group in 1969, but in 1996 there is no relationship between the share of earnings from manufacturing and size of place. Neither the primary production group nor the advanced consumer services group shows any relationship between their shares of earnings and metropolitan size (see Table 4.2).

5. Does the level of human capital positively affect the level of metropolitan income? None of the estimated equations for the level of per capita personal income includes the human capital variable, because of its high correlation with the share of earnings from other producer services, and so the analysis presented does not answer this question. However, the simple correlation between per capita income and the human capital variable, measured by the percentage of adults with at least a college degree, is large and positive in 1996 but small and positive in 1969. Thus, the magnitude of the effect increases over time (see Table 4.4).

6. Do specialization and human capital affect metropolitan income growth? Specialization in either broad sector of traded goods and services, goods production and distribution or information, at the beginning of the periods analyzed enhances subsequent growth in real per capita income. However, in the short period (1969–79) the effect is smaller for the information sector and virtually absent for the goods production and distribution sector. A high initial level of human capital boosts subsequent growth of per capita income, but not in the short period, 1969–79 (see Table 4.10).

7. Do size, specialization, and human capital affect metropolitan population growth and metropolitan employment growth? Initial size has a moderate negative effect on metropolitan population growth over the long period, 1969–96, and the first short period, 1969–79. It has almost no effect in the second short period, 1979–96. Initial specialization in manufacturing or distribution has large negative effects upon subsequent population growth, 1969–96, although specialization in the primary production group has a positive effect. Initial specialization in financial or other producer services has large positive effects upon subsequent population growth, while initial specialization in advanced consumer services adds very little to population growth. When the two broad sectors of specialization rather than the six individual groups are included in population growth equations, the effects are consistent. That is, initial specialization in the goods production and distribution sector substantially reduces subsequent population growth, whereas initial specialization in the information sector raises subsequent population growth. The additions to population growth from the information sector are considerably smaller than the reductions in population growth from the goods production and distribution sector (see Table 4.10). The

initial level of human capital was never a significant variable in any population growth equations and so was not included.

Employment growth, unlike population growth, is positively affected by initial human capital, measured by college attainment. Initial size, measured by total employment, has a large negative effect on subsequent employment growth, except in the most recent period, 1979–96, when it has no effect. As with population growth, initial specialization in manufacturing and distribution has large negative effects on subsequent employment growth, while initial specialization in the two producer services groups has large positive effects. Initial specialization in either the primary production or the advanced consumer services groups has small positive effects on employment growth. When the shares are aggregated into the two sectors, goods production and distribution, and information, the effects are consistent: negative for goods production and distribution and positive for information.

To sum up this chapter in one pithy sound bite is challenging. The degree of metropolitan specialization rises with population size for some groups (distribution and the two producer services) but not for the others. Specialization generally improves the level of per capita income, except for specialization in distribution. Specialization in either of the two producer service groups raises the level of per capita income more than specialization in manufacturing, while specialization in advanced consumer services contributes less to the level of per capita income than specialization in manufacturing. Higher levels of human capital add to growth in metropolitan per capita income. Specialization in either of the two broad sectors also adds to growth in per capita income. Population growth is greatly reduced by initial specialization in goods production and distribution and less greatly enhanced by initial specialization in information. Employment growth is also reduced by initial specialization in goods production and distribution, but less so. Initial specialization in information adds about as much to growth as the other sector subtracts from growth. Higher levels of human capital at the beginning of a period enhance subsequent employment growth. Not pithy perhaps, but important for understanding sources of economic development of metropolitan economies.

5 | Income Convergence and Poverty in Metropolitan Areas

Two issues remain to be addressed. The first is income convergence, that is, the hypothesized tendency for incomes in metropolitan areas to become closer together over long time spans. Whether in fact they do or not is a question I have addressed elsewhere with José Lobo (1999 and forthcoming). The importance of income convergence for this study is, first, to show that divergence has replaced convergence over the past quarter-century and, then, to determine if the places characterized by income diverging *up* are different from the places characterized by income diverging *down*. The differences of interest, given all that has come before, are specialization, human capital, and size.

The second issue addressed in this chapter is urban poverty. There is an extensive literature which claims that the rise in urban poverty observed in U.S. cities over the past thirty years is the result of the transformation from urban economies specialized in goods production and distribution to economies specialized in information. It may be true, as William Julius Wilson (1996) has carefully documented for Chicago, that the disappearance of manufacturing jobs in cities has contributed to a rise in urban poverty. But it may not be true that the simultaneous rise of the information sector in urban areas has exacerbated or even contributed to that rise in poverty.

Are Metropolitan Incomes Converging or Diverging?

Income convergence means that places with higher than average income will tend to have long-term income growth that is slower than average, and places with lower than average income will tend to have long-term income growth that is faster than average. In the long run, relative income differences among places will become smaller, that is, incomes will converge. The income convergence hypothesis arises from the neoclassical economic model, which assumes unrestricted mobility of labor and capital. Places where labor is relatively abundant will tend to have lower wages than places where labor is relatively scarce. Similarly, places where capital is relatively abundant will tend to have lower returns to capital than places where capital is relatively scarce. Labor in low-wage places will tend to migrate to higher-wage places, while owners of capital will tend to relocate their capital from low-return places to higher-return places. Thus, the model argues that differences in returns to labor or capital among different places will diminish over time. The hypothesis is more plausible for places within a nation than among nations, because of the mobility assumption and because property rights, language, currency, and customs are more homogeneous. In the 1960s, the convergence hypothesis was tested for states (Borts 1960; Borts and Stein 1964) and for regions (Perloff 1963) of the United States. Their results mostly supported income convergence, but with some exceptions.

That might have been the end of the story had it not been for evidence of income divergence (the opposite of convergence) among states and regions of the United States in the 1980s. Beginning in the late 1980s, there has been a flurry of articles in the economics literature testing for convergence using regions, states, and metropolitan areas as the units of analysis (see for example Barro and Sala-I-Martin 1991; Blanchard and Katz 1992; Drennan and Lobo 1999 and forthcoming; Drennan, Tobier, and Lewis 1996; Garnick 1990; Glaeser, Scheinkman, and Shleifer 1995). Most of them found some evidence of divergence in the 1980s. The most thorough of these studies, by Barro and Sala-I-Martin, covered 110 years, using state per capita income data. Their results support convergence except for during two decades: the 1920s and the 1980s. They dismiss these exceptions as aberrations that were due to factors that did or would likely disappear. They carefully distinguish two types of convergence. The first, as defined above (richer places grow more slowly, poorer places grow faster) they label "beta convergence." The second type, "sigma convergence," is the tendency for the variation of income among places to diminish over time. Variation is measured by the standard deviation of income divided by the mean income for all places for a year. That measure is called the coefficient of variation. If over

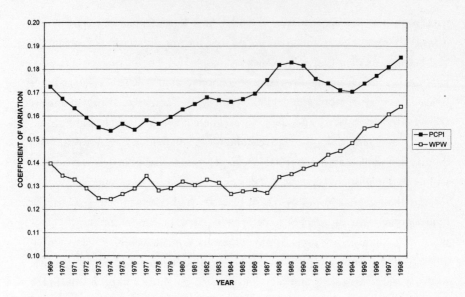

Figure 5.1 Variation in U.S. Metropolitan per Capita Personal Income and Wage per Worker, 1969–1998

time it shows a downward trend, then that supports convergence. If it shows an upward trend, that supports divergence. Milton Friedman (1992) has argued that sigma convergence (diminished dispersion over time) is the only valid measure of whether incomes are converging or not.

In a recent article that I wrote with José Lobo (forthcoming), we calculated the coefficient of variation of per capita personal income and of the annual average wage for all metropolitan areas for every year from 1969 through 1998. Figure 5.1 presents the plots of those two variables. Over such a long time period, 30 years, if the theory of income convergence is correct, one would see a downward trend in both variables. For the per capita personal income coefficient of variation, the first six years or so do show a downward trend. But then, from the mid-1970s through the entire 1980s, the variable rises. From 1989 through 1994, which includes the last recession, it declines somewhat but then resumes its upward trend, 1994–98. The 1998 value of 18.5% is higher than any of the earlier years shown and three percentage points above the low of 15.4% in 1974. The clear presence of an upward trend argues against sigma convergence of metropolitan per capita income.

Although the pattern is somewhat different for the coefficient of variation of the average annual wage for metropolitan areas, the conclusion is the same. That variable declined for the first five years and then was more or less flat from 1975 through 1987. Since then, it has been rising every year, even during the recession of the early 1990s. The 1998 value of 16.4% is higher than for any other year shown and is four percentage points higher than the low of 12.4% in 1974. Thus, the visual evidence does not support sigma convergence for average annual earnings either. A visual examination is not as persuasive as a formal statistical test, however, and in the article we applied a unit root test to both data series of Figure 5.1 in order to rigorously test for sigma convergence. The test results indicated that each data series can be characterized as a random walk with positive drift. That means that neither one has a downward trend and therefore neither one exhibits convergence.

Of course, one could argue that both per capita personal income and average annual earnings are too coarse-grained to test the income convergence hypothesis. Perhaps a better measure would be full-time earnings of year-round workers. But if that is the case, then all of the earlier studies supporting convergence would also have to be discounted, because they use the same sort of coarse-grained measures I use here. If the observed divergence, the opposite of convergence, reflects the fact that metropolitan areas have become more dissimilar in their proportions of full-time year-round workers, that itself would suggest that metropolitan areas are becoming more dissimilar in the strength of their economies.

There may be a connection between the much noted rising income inequality in the United States and the absence of convergence in per capita income and average earnings among metropolitan areas. The new information economy that seems to favor large places specialized in financial and other producer services, places with high levels of human capital, may be one cause of the observed lack of convergence. Indeed, rising income inequality may have an important spatial component, but that is not an issue taken up in this book.

I have argued throughout this book that the economic fortunes of metropolitan areas are tied to their traded goods and services specializations and to their human capital, as measured by adults with college or higher educations. The evidence presented in Chapters 3 and 4 indicates that specialization affects both the level and the growth of income and that some specializations are better than others for some time periods. Also, it appears that large places tend to be more specialized than small places and tend to have specializations that are better in the modern economy, namely financial producer services and other producer services (see Table 3.4). In other words, specialization, size, and human capital all appear to affect the level and growth of metropolitan income. So convergence or its absence may be associated with specialization, size, and human capital.

To explore that issue, I have sorted the 273 metropolitan areas into four mutually exclusive and exhaustive categories, a procedure that José Lobo and I developed in our first paper on convergence (1999) in order to test for beta convergence (richer places grow more slowly and poorer places grow faster). My purpose here is not to test for beta convergence but rather to determine if places that *do not* converge are similar or different in a number of characteristics, most importantly in specialization, size, and human capital. The four categories are:

1. Per capita income in 1969 above metropolitan average and per capita income growth 1969–96 below metropolitan average growth
2. Per capita income in 1969 below metropolitan average and per capita income growth 1969–96 above metropolitan average growth
3. Per capita income in 1969 above metropolitan average and per capita income growth 1969–96 *above* metropolitan average growth
4. Per capita income in 1969 below metropolitan average and per capita income growth 1969–96 *below* metropolitan average growth

The first two categories correspond to convergence, and the second two correspond to divergence. Number three means richer places grow faster (winners), and number four means poorer places grow more slowly (losers). I am only interested in categories 3 and 4. Of the 273 metropolitan areas sorted into the four categories, 46 fall into category 3, the winners, and 48 fall into category 4, the losers. The characteristics of the winners (diverging up) and losers (diverging down) are summarized in Table 5.1.

The winners are far larger than the losers, with a median population of 808,000 compared with 152,000 for the losers. Of the 46 winners, 20 have populations above one million. Only one of the losers is above one million (Norfolk–Virginia Beach–Newport News, Virginia). Most of the losers are quite small: 33 out of 48 have populations of 250,000 or less. Only 11 of the winners are that small. The winners are much more likely to be specialized (as defined

Table 5.1. Characteristics of Metropolitan Areas with Diverging Trends
in per Capita Personal Income, 1969–1996

Characteristics	Diverging Up (Winners)	Diverging Down (Losers)
Number of metropolitan areas	46	48
Population (thousands)		
Total	88,427	11,800
Mean	1,922	246
Median	808	152
Minimum	100	57
Maximum	19,800	1,536
Number with populations of one million or more	20	1
Number with populations of 250,000 or less	11	33
Specialization		
Number with 2 or more specializations	11	1
Number with 1 specialization	27	20
Number with no specializations	8	27
Number with a specialization in		
Primary production	1	4
Manufacturing	4	3
Distribution	9	4
Financial producer services	17	1
Other producer services	12	1
Advanced consumer services	7	9
Percent of adults with college degrees or more in 1990		
Mean	23.2%	16.9%
Number of places with percent >19.6, metro. mean	33	11
Number of places with percent < or = 19.6, metro. mean	13	37
Minimum percent	13.6%	9.5%
Maximum percent	35.7%	35.8%
Central city poverty rate, 1995	17.4%	20.0%
Region		
Sunbelt (South and West)	19	38
Snowbelt (Northeast and Midwest)	27	10

Source: Computed from BEA 1998a. College attainment from 1990 census, and poverty data
from U.S. Department of Housing and Urban Development 1999.
Note: Characteristics are for 1996 unless otherwise noted.

here) in traded goods and services groups than are the losers. Eleven of the winners have two or more specializations, while only one of the losers has two or
more specializations. Twenty-seven other winners have one specialization while
20 of the losers have one specialization. More than half (27) of the losers have
no specialization, while only eight of the winners are without specializations.

The winners and losers differ not only in the number of specializations but
also in the type of specialization. Four of the losers are specialized in the primary
production group and nine are specialized in advanced consumer services. Those

are the only two groups in which the losers outnumber the winners. Three of the losers are specialized in manufacturing compared with four of the winners. Four of the losers are specialized in distribution, while nine of the winners are so specialized. The striking differences are in the two producer services groups. Among the winners, 17 are specialized in financial producer services, and 12 are specialized in other producer services. The losers have only one in each of those groups.

The two sets of places differ markedly on the human capital characteristic too. Among the winners, 23% of the adult population have college degrees or more, while among the losers 17% do. The metropolitan mean of 20% with college or more is exceeded by 33 of the winners and only 11 of the losers. The old and popular Sunbelt-Snowbelt dichotomy does not fare well in this comparison. Far more of the winners (27) are in the Snowbelt than in the Sunbelt (19). Far more of the losers are in the Sunbelt (38) than in the Snowbelt (10). (The lists of winners and losers and some of their characteristics are in "Supplementary Tables" 2002, Table S22). The usual suspects are among the winners: Atlanta, Boston, Charlotte, Dallas, Denver, Houston, Minneapolis, New York, San Francisco, Santa Fe, and Washington. But there are surprises among the winners too, such as Allentown, Cincinnati, Columbus, Des Moines, Hartford, Louisville, New London, Philadelphia, Pittsburgh, and St. Louis. The four places specialized in manufacturing among the winners are Appleton-Oshkosh, Wisconsin; Grand Rapids, Michigan; Greensboro–Winston-Salem, North Carolina; and Kokomo, Indiana. The last is also the most specialized in manufacturing of all metropolitan areas, with 65% of its earnings from manufacturing (the minimum share for classification as specialized in manufacturing in 1996 is 29%).

One characteristic that distinguishes the winners from the losers is the percent of central city dwellers that have incomes below the poverty level. The poverty data from the U.S. Department of Housing and Urban Development (1999) are for the central city or cities of the metropolitan areas, not for the entire metropolitan area. For metropolitan areas with two or more central cities, the poverty rate is the weighted average (weighted by central city population) of the poverty rates for all the central cities in that metropolitan area. For all the central cities of the 273 metropolitan areas included here, the simple average of the poverty rate is 19.0% for 1995. For the losers it is higher, 20.0%; for the winners it is lower, 17.4%. That may not seem to show much difference, but in fact it does. I have computed a confidence interval for the metropolitanwide mean. It ranges from 19.8% to 18.1%, indicating that a random sample of metropolitan areas from the entire set would most likely (with 95% probability) have an average poverty rate within that range. The fact that the winners are well below that range, 17.4%, while the losers are slightly above that range, 20.0%, argues that those two sets of places are indeed different from each other and different from the set of all places in percentage of residents living in poverty. Despite the fact that larger metropolitan areas tend to have higher poverty rates, as shown below, the winners, although decidedly larger than the losers (see Table 5.1), have significantly lower poverty rates.

Compared with the losers, the winners are much larger, have significantly lower poverty rates, significantly higher levels of human capital, are more likely to be specialized, and are far more likely to be specialized in one of the two producer services groups. Those facts raise the question What is the importance, if any, of past employment growth, specialization, human capital, and size, for the economic well-being of low-income persons in metropolitan areas?

Are Metropolitan Economies Specialized in the Information Sector Bad for the Poor?

The percentage of persons in the United States that had income below the poverty level in 1960 was 22%. In the subsequent ten years, that rate dropped almost ten percentage points. Since 1970 however, it has mostly moved back up, fluctuating between 11% and 15% (U.S. Census Bureau 1999). The persistence of poverty, its spatial concentration in large cities and in rural areas, not in suburbs, and its higher incidence among minority populations has generated an enormous quantity of social science literature. In the urban literature addressing poverty, two facts are widely noted that are not contested. First, from 1970 to 1990 the number of poor persons in metropolitan areas grew faster than total metropolitan populations, and those central city areas characterized by high rates of poverty expanded (Jargowsky 1997). Second, the number of blue-collar manufacturing jobs in central cities of metropolitan areas dropped sharply from 1970 to 1990. From those two facts, some authors have inferred that the disappearance of manufacturing jobs from cities is the major cause of increased poverty in cities, particularly among blacks. But the more careful econometric analyses of that issue, reviewed by Jargowsky (1997), lead him to conclude, "All things considered, the early emphasis of researchers on manufacturing may have been misplaced. There is, at best, only modest evidence to support the notion that the shift from manufacturing to services is important to the overall poverty rate of blacks, and almost no direct evidence that it contributes to the growth of poor neighborhoods" (p. 122).

Is the expansion of an urban information economy bad for low-income and low-skilled people? Saskia Sassen answers maybe not in the new edition of her noteworthy book, *The Global City* (2001), which is about the dominance of an internationally oriented producer services sector in New York, London, and Tokyo. "Perhaps most important is the fact that compared to other cities, global city status does not necessarily represent the disadvantage for the bottom stratum that I had postulated in the first edition. . . . being in a global city may not be all that bad for low-income workers, compared to being in other types of cities" (p. 249). Sassen's change of view on that question is based in part upon a number of studies released after her first edition was published in 1991.

One critique of the view that an urban information economy is bad for the poor that I find persuasive is that of the geographer Michael Storper (1997). In a comparison of New York and Los Angeles with the United States as a whole, Storper shows that from 1979 to 1989, the proportion of households in the bottom classes of the income distribution showed improvement (reduction) in those two metropolitan areas while it did not improve in the nation: "Indeed, . . . with respect to household-income inequality trends in the two biggest American cities—frequently cited in the literature on dualism as exemplary cases of urban economic polarization—the lower tail of the distribution actually declined more in these big cities than in the American economy in general, while the upper tail grew more in those cities. This appearance of polarization is false: the whole distribution followed a more generally more upward direction than in the economy as a whole, hardly the catastrophic picture painted by the global–dual city theory" (pp. 230–32). Both New York and Los Angeles are specialized in producer services (see Table 3.6). In a recent study of New York compared with London, using the decennial census data on income distribution in the New York CMSA for 1979 and 1989, I arrived at the same conclusion as Storper, namely, that there was an upward shift in the entire distribution that was not mirrored in the national data (Drennan 2000a).

Nonetheless, the view persists that the postindustrial urban economy that has developed in New York has hurt low-income people. In the introduction to an edited collection on London and New York, *Divided Cities* (Fainstein, Gordon, and Harloe 1992), Fainstein and Harloe assert the same: "Harking back to the England of Disraeli's two nations and Jacob Riis's other half, many commentators on these processes [transformation to a producer services urban economy] have identified a social duality wherein one part of the population experienced affluence and success while the other suffered degradation. Economic growth in both cities has been accompanied by sharp increases at both the top and bottom ends of the income distribution" (p. 7). As noted above, the census income distributions for New York for 1979 and 1989 show a reduction in the proportion of households in the bottom end of the income distribution. I have no doubt that income polarization, measured by the ratio of income in the highest income class to that in the lowest income class, did in fact increase, as Mollenkopf and Castells have shown (1991). But that does not mean that the proportion of households in the bottom class went up. In one of the pieces in *Divided Cities*, Logan, Taylor-Gooby, and Reuter state, "In the early 1980s civic boosters assumed that if [London and New York] could successfully manage the transition from a manufacturing to a service-based economy, general prosperity would result. . . . It quickly became apparent, however, that growth in property development and advanced services did not improve the situation of the bottom quartile of the population" (p. 127). But a table two pages later in the article shows that, although real household income in New York in the bottom quartile declined from 1977 to 1983, during the subsequent three years, 1983–86, it rose by far more than enough to offset the previous decline.

A more recent example of the opinion that an urban information economy is bad for the poor is the edited collection by Peter Marcuse and Ronald van Kempen, *Globalizing Cities: A New Spatial Order?* (2000). In the introduction, the editors note: "Globalization clearly has much to do with mobility of goods, of capital, of persons. . . . One of the main changes in Western societies . . . has been, and still is, the declining importance of manufacturing, and the increasing significance of services" (p. 5). Then they address the consequences of that shift for the urban poor: "For the very poor, by the same token, their spatially defined neighborhoods, while in ways growing even more important for their residents, become more and more irrelevant to the functioning of the mainstream economy." Further, they identify "globalization as leading to a kind of socio-economic symbiosis within an increasingly polarized society, which can be seen in a growing number of highly educated, wealthy persons and households, but also in an increasing number of people in the lower segments of the economy (in dead-end jobs and chronically unemployed)" (p. 7). Marcuse and van Kempen then assert that a wholly new type of poor neighborhood has evolved in postindustrial cities: "But a new urban ghetto is developing, under the polarizing impact of current economic changes; we call it the the excluded ghetto. It may be defined as 'a ghetto in which race or ethnicity is combined with class in a spatially concentrated area whose residents are excluded from the economic life of the surrounding society, which does not profit significantly from its existence'" (p. 19). Two of the contributors to that collection argue that the transformation of an urban area from goods production to information entails far more losses than gains: "The shrinkage of the manufacturing sector left behind hollowed-out industrial landscapes and the new economic base compensated for neither the properties nor the jobs that were lost" (Beauregard and Haila 2000, p. 25). The picture painted is indeed bleak. The transformation of an urban economy from goods production to information is neither painless nor smooth, and it may well produce wrenching human dislocations (Mollenkopf and Castells 1991). But I do not believe that an expanding urban information economy leads to both an increasing number of poor neighborhoods and increasing number of those in misery and penury. The editors, Marcuse and van Kempen (2000), do believe that. In their conclusion, they note the spatial manifestations of the change from the old economy of goods to the new economy of information, referring to the "quarters of those excluded from the globalizing economy, with their residents more and more isolated and walled in" (p. 271).

With the exceptions of Sassen (2001) and Storper (1997), a common theme among the authors quoted above is that an information economy is bad for low-income, low-skilled people. If that is the case, one would expect to see greater economic hardship in places specialized in the information sector compared with places not so specialized. One broad measure of economic hardship is the percentage of persons with incomes below the poverty level. The urban poor tend to be concentrated in the central cities of metropolitan areas, particularly in the larger central cities. I have calculated poverty rates for each metropolitan area from the HUD poverty rates for cities in 1995 (U.S. Department of Housing and

Table 5.2. Central City Poverty Rates, by Type
of Metropolitan Area, 1995

	Percentage of Persons in Poverty, Central Cities
All metropolitan areas	19.0
Specialized metropolitan areas	
Primary	20.3
Manufacturing	18.9
Distribution	18.8
Financial producer services	16.7
Other producer services	18.0
Advanced consumer services	19.5
Nonspecialized metropolitan areas	19.5

Source: Calculated from individual city poverty data in U.S.
Department of Housing and Urban Development 1999.

Urban Development 1999) (Table 5.2). The figure I cite is the weighted average of the poverty rates for the central cities included in the metropolitan area. If there is only one central city, then it is simply the HUD poverty rate for that city. Contrary to the view expressed above that an information economy is bad for low-income, low-skilled workers, it appears that places specialized in either financial producer services or other producer services have significantly lower poverty rates, 16.7% and 18.0% respectively, than the average for all metropolitan areas, 19.0%. The third group of the information sector, advanced consumer services, has a poverty rate of 19.5%, which, although higher, is not significantly different from the metropolitan average of 19.0%. Poverty rates for places specialized in manufacturing (18.9%) or distribution (18.8%) are likewise not significantly different from the average for all metropolitan areas. The same is the case for the set of places that have no specializations. It is only places specialized in the primary production group that have a poverty rate (20.3%) significantly above the metropolitan average.

The poverty rates for 1995 provide a snapshot that enables a comparison among the different types of places at one point in time. They provide no information about changes in poverty or poverty populations over time. Paul Jargowsky, in his book *Poverty and Place* (1997), developed an unambiguous definition of high-poverty neighborhoods in metropolitan areas, using census tracts as the basic spatial unit. He measured the numbers of such neighborhoods and their populations for the census years 1970, 1980, and 1990. The data show that, while the U.S. population in metropolitan areas increased 28% from 1970 to 1990, the population living in high-poverty neighborhoods in metropolitan areas soared, by 92%. The biggest gain was in the decade of the 1980s, 54%. Interestingly, the big rise in population in high-poverty neighborhoods was not spread evenly over all metropolitan areas. Metropolitan areas specialized in the goods production and distribution sector had a 134% increase in populations living in high-poverty neighborhoods. Metropolitan areas specialized in the information sector only had a 30% increase. Nonspecialized metropolitan areas showed a 65% increase. The individual groups of specialized places had widely different percentage increases (no group had a decline). The places specialized in manufacturing had a 192% increase in population in high-poverty neighborhoods, while places specialized in other producer services had a 44% rise. The smallest rise was for places specialized in financial producer services, 8%, and the largest rise was for places specialized in the primary production group, 387% (Table 5.3). Not all information sector groups had below average (54%) increases. The places specialized in advanced consumer services had a 102% rise. The substantial increases do not mean that such neighborhoods were increasing in density, but rather that the number of such neighborhoods, census tracts, had increased in most cities.

Although the places classified as specialized in the financial producer services and other producer services groups of the information sector had the smallest

Table 5.3. Population in High-Poverty Neighborhoods, by Type of Metropolitan Area, 1980 and 1990
(thousands)

	1980	1990	Change (%)
All metropolitan areas	5,174	7,973	54
Specialized metropolitan areas			
Primary production (11)	45	219	387
Manufacturing (31)	262	765	192
Distribution (22)	452	791	75
TOTAL GOODS PRODUCTION AND DISTRIBUTION	759	1,775	134
Financial producer services (21)	1,606	1,734	8
Other producer services (26)	1,252	1,808	44
Advanced consumer services (19)	229	463	102
TOTAL INFORMATION	3,087	4,005	30
Nonspecialized metropolitan areas	1,328	2,193	65

Source: Jargowsky 1997, Table 2.2, p. 38, and Appendix Table B.1, pp. 222–32.
Note: Numbers in parentheses indicate the number of metropolitan areas in each group for which the poverty neighborhood population was available from Jargowsky.

percentage gains in population living in high-poverty neighborhoods, they had far higher absolute numbers of people living in those neighborhoods than any other group in both 1980 and 1990, and their numbers increased during those ten years. There were 1.7 million people living in high-poverty central city neighborhoods in places specialized in financial producer services in 1990, compared with 1.6 million in 1980. For places specialized in other producer services the 1990 total was 1.8 million compared with 1.3 million in 1980. None of the other four groups of specialized places had anywhere close to such high numbers. The nonspecialized places, however, had comparable numbers: 2.2 million in 1990 and 1.3 million in 1980. The reason that the two producer service group places have so much higher numbers, I believe, is that they tend to be much larger places, as I have shown (see Tables 3.4 and 3.5). Although their populations in high poverty neighborhoods are indeed much larger than in the other groups of specialized places, their poverty rates are significantly lower than the metropolitan average, as shown in Table 5.2. As Jargowsky (1997) argues, "neighborhood poverty is largely determined by the overall economic conditions prevailing in a metropolitan area and the levels of segregation by race and income" (p. 6).

Jargowsky supports that argument with a sophisticated logit regression model in which the log-odds of neighborhood poverty for various minority populations are related to metropolitan area measures of income and income inequality, the share of employment in manufacturing, the share of employment in professional occupations, measures of segregation, and regional dummy variables. The model is estimated for a sample of 116 metropolitan areas for 1970, 1980, and 1990. His results for 1990 indicate that the higher the share of jobs in manufacturing in the metropolitan area the greater the likelihood of neighborhood poverty, while the higher the share of jobs in professional occupations the lower the likelihood of neighborhood poverty, although neither of those variables is significant. Higher mean income of the metropolitan area , however, always lowers the likelihood of neighborhood poverty, and the income variable is highly significant in all of his equations. That result undercuts the views cited above that the economic fortunes of the poor in cities are impervious to the level of metropolitan income, and indeed may even be hurt by a high-income postindustrial economy.

The data of Tables 5.2 and 5.3 suggest that metropolitan areas that are specialized in two of the three information sector groups, financial and other pro-

ducer services, have lower poverty rates and lower growth in poverty populations in their central cities than do metropolitan areas with other specializations
or with no specialization. Jargowsky's results indicate that higher metropolitan
income reduces neighborhood poverty, and that specialization in manufacturing
has no significant effect. In the context of this study, those results raise the question What is the effect of metropolitan specialization, human capital, and size
upon poverty in cities?

To address that question, I have estimated a number of ordinary least squares
regression equations in which the percentage of central city population below
the poverty level is the dependent variable. This analysis must be considered ex-
ploratory, because I do not have a formal model that takes into account the in-
terdependence among some of the variables or that addresses the important
question of why poverty might shrink or expand over time. As noted, I have calculated the central city or cities 1995 percentage of persons in poverty for all 269
metropolitan areas used in this study. The explanatory variables are defined in
Chapter 4. Problems of endogeneity and multicolinearity noted in Chapter 4 require that I not include all explanatory variables in a single equation. The specification of the three equations I have estimated is as follows.

$$
\begin{aligned}
LCCPOV95_{(i)} = {} & a_{(0)} + a_{(1)}LPOP96_{(i)} + a_{(2)}LDEMP7996_{(i)} \\
& + a_{(3)}SOUTH_{(i)} + a_{(4)}MFGSH96_{(i)} + a_{(5)}DISTSH96_{(i)} \\
& + a_{(6)}PSFINSH96_{(i)} + a_{(7)}PSOTHSH96_{(i)} + a_{(8)}ACSSH96_{(i)} + e_{(i)}
\end{aligned}
\quad (5.1)
$$

$$
\begin{aligned}
LCCPOV95_{(i)} = {} & b_{(0)} + b_{(1)}LPOP96_{(i)} + b_{(2)}LDEMP7996_{(i)} \\
& + b_{(3)}SOUTH_{(i)} + b_{(4)}COLL90_{(i)} + e_{(i)}
\end{aligned}
\quad (5.2)
$$

$$
\begin{aligned}
LCCPOV95_{(i)} = {} & c_{(0)} + c_{(1)}LPOP96_{(i)} + c_{(2)}LDEMP7996_{(i)} \\
& + c_{(3)}SOUTH_{(i)} + c_{(4)}LPCPI96_{(i)} + e_{(i)}
\end{aligned}
\quad (5.3)
$$

In all three equations the dependent variable is the natural log of the central
city or cities percentage of population in poverty in 1995. All three equations
have on the right-hand side a measure of the size of the metropolitan area, the
log of population in 1996 (LPOP96), metropolitan employment growth from
1979 to 1996 (LDEMP7996), and the regional dummy variable indicating
whether the metropolitan area is located in the south or not (SOUTH). Equation
(5.1) also has the metropolitan share of earnings in five of the six specialization

Table 5.4. Regression Estimates: Logarithm of Central City Poverty Rate, 1995

	LCCPOV95	LCCPOV95	LCCPOV95
Intercept	2.4275	2.5567	11.8946
	(15.6)	(22.8)	(9.6)
LPOP96	0.1471	0.1050	0.1653
	(6.0)	(5.9)	(8.9)
LDEMP7996	−0.3097	−0.4291	−0.5383
	(4.6)	(3.8)	(5.7)
SOUTH	0.2165	0.2118	0.1668
	(5.5)	(5.3)	(4.5)
COLL90	—	−0.0124	—
		(3.5)	
LPCPI96	—	—	−0.9994
			(7.7)
MFGSH96	−0.5552	—	—
	(2.4)		
DISTSH96	0.1559	—	—
	(0.2)		
PSFINSH96	−2.2142	—	—
	(2.8)		
PSOTHSH96	−1.6573	—	—
	(2.4)		
ACSSH96	0.6137	—	—
	(1.1)		
adj. R^2	0.25	0.24	0.35
F statistic	11.9	22.6	37.7
n	269	269	269

Source: Calculated for this study from BEA 1998a and U.S. Department of Housing and Urban Development 1999.

Note: Absolute values of t statistics in parentheses.

categories. The primary production group share of metropolitan earnings is excluded because it is not even close to significance. Equation (5.2) adds in the human capital measure, the percent of adults in the metropolitan area with at least a college degree in 1990 (COLL90), and excludes all of the measures of specialization. Equation (5.3) adds in one of the most important variables in Jargowsky's analysis, the log of metropolitan per capita income (LPCPI96), and excludes the human capital variable (COLL90) as well as excluding the five specialization variables. The estimated regressions are presented in Table 5.4.

The three variables that appear in all three equations, size (LPOP96), past employment growth (LDEMP7996), and the regional dummy (SOUTH), are always highly significant (the lowest t statistic is 3.8) and always have the expected signs. The size variable is positive, indicating that larger metropolitan areas tend to have higher rates of central city poverty. The past employment growth variable is negative, indicating that past employment growth of the metropolitan area reduces central city poverty. Being located in the south increases a central city's rate of poverty. Equation (5.1), which includes the five shares of earnings in each traded goods and services specialization group, shows that three of the groups have negative, significant relationships with central city poverty, that is, the higher the share of metropolitan earnings in any of those three, the lower the rate of central city poverty. Those three are manufacturing (MFGSH96), financial producer services (PSFINSH96), and other producer services (PSOTH96). Note that the negative coefficient on the financial producer services share is four times larger than the negative coefficient on the manufacturing share, and the negative coefficient on the other producer services share is three times larger. The shares of metropolitan earnings in distribution (DISTSH96) and advanced consumer services (ACSSH96) are both positive but insignificant, suggesting that they have no effect on central city poverty. The adjusted R^2 of equation (5.1) is 0.25.

Equation (5.2) drops all of the specialization measures and adds the human capital variable (COLL90). It is negative and highly significant, indicating that higher rates of college educated people in the metropolitan area reduce central city poverty. The adjusted R^2 is 0.24.

Equation (5.3) drops the human capital variable (COLL90) and adds the log of metropolitan per capita personal income in 1996 (LPCPI96). No specialization variables are included. Not surprisingly, to me at least, that equation has the highest adjusted R^2, 0.35. The metropolitan per capita income variable has a negative coefficient that is highly significant ($t = 7.7$), indicating that when the per capita income of a metropolitan area is higher, central city poverty rates will be lower. Because both the dependent variable and the per capita income variable are in log form, the coefficient on per capita income can be interpreted as an elasticity. Its value, -0.9994, indicates that a 1% increase in metropolitan per capita income reduces the central city poverty rate by 1%. I must emphasize that that does *not* refer to growth over time but reflects the fact that metropolitan areas with higher *levels* of per capita income tend to have lower rates of central city poverty.

The central message conveyed by this analysis is that central city poverty is *not* impervious to economic conditions of the wider metropolitan area. The poor are not sealed off in a separate world. If city poverty rates are lower where metropolitan employment growth is higher, then the poor must be among the beneficiaries of that growth. If city poverty rates tend to be 1% lower when metropolitan per capita personal income is 1% higher than average, then the poor must gain from living in places with higher metropolitan income. Similarly, they gain from being in metropolitan areas with higher levels of college attainment. As Sassen (2001) asserts, a strong manufacturing economy is good for lower-income people, and the fact that higher shares of metropolitan earnings in manufacturing are associated with lower city poverty rates lends support to her claim. But the view that a producer service economy is bad for such low-income people is not supported by these findings. Indeed, the opposite appears to be the case, namely, city poverty rates are lower in metropolitan areas with higher shares of earnings in financial and other producer services. Another view of city poverty that is called into question by these (and Jargowsky's) results is that of the Brookings urban economist, Anthony Downs. He argues that as metropolitan areas expand in population and territory and as the poverty rate fluctuates cyclically and as the poor are confined to the inner city, then inevitably the absolute number of poor will rise in the central cities. Assuming that the city population does not grow, then the rate of city poverty will also rise (Downs 1997). That grim picture implicitly assumes no role for the specific economic circumstances of the metropolitan area as opposed to the general economic effects of business cycle expansions, which reduce poverty rates, and contractions, which raise them. But as shown above, city poverty rates do respond to the specific economic conditions of metropolitan areas.

During the first Clinton campaign for the presidency, in 1992, it was reported that desks at the campaign headquarters had a sign saying "It's the economy, stupid." In light of this analysis and the study by Jargowsky (1997), I think that all the nonprofit community development corporations working in inner cities and all the municipal agencies charged with improving the life chances for the city poor should have the same sign in their offices.

6 | Conclusion and
Policy Recommendations

Conclusion

Large metropolitan areas that are specialized in financial or other producer services, two of the three groups of the information sector, appear to be the more economically successful urban areas at the end of the twentieth century. It does not matter if they are in the Sunbelt or Snowbelt. It does not matter if they are old (Boston) or young (Dallas). It does matter if they are specialized. Specialization seems to promote stronger economies than does diversity, with all the qualifications and exceptions noted. Most metropolitan areas are specialized in at least one of the six traded goods and services groups. But specialization is not a static characteristic; rather, it is dynamic. The number of places specialized in any group has changed over time, and that change is tied to shifts in the composition of national output or GDP. The increasing relative importance of the information sector in GDP quite naturally has been accompanied by increases in the number of metropolitan areas specialized in the three information sector groups. At the same time, the decreasing relative importance of the goods production and distribution sector in GDP has been accompanied by declines in the number of metropolitan areas specialized in the three goods production and distribution groups. High levels of human capital, represented by college attainment, also promote stronger metropolitan economies, and no qualifications or exceptions seem to apply to that variable. Size of the metropolitan area, as measured in population, matters too. Large size seems to be linked with specialization in financial and other producer services. That was not always the case. Large size is not characteristic of places specialized in manufacturing. Large size is characteristic of places with above average income, and above average long-term growth of income. Income divergence among metropolitan areas has become the norm over the past quarter-century, not the exception. It may be linked to size, specialization, and human capital, and so it may not disappear in the coming years. Poverty in cities is not made worse by a "yuppie" economy specialized in producer services. Indeed, it may be lowered. Although the population living in poor neighborhoods of central cities rose sharply from 1980 to 1990, examining the cities by specialization group reveals large differences. Again, it is the metropolitan areas specialized in financial and other producer services that had the lowest percentage increases in populations living in poor neighborhoods. And the nonspecialized or diversified places had above average increases in such populations.

One large question is not addressed by this study. First, what is the effect, if any, of specialization upon the distribution of income in metropolitan areas? Janice Madden (2000) has carefully analyzed intrametropolitan income distribution over time using census data. The most recent year in her study is 1989, before the boom of the 1990s that has worsened, that is, made more unequal, the national distribution of income. Even if her data made possible a comparison of income distributions among places grouped by specialization, which it does not, it would not be satisfactory. The decade of the 1990s must be included in any analysis of the effect of specialization in the information sector upon metropolitan income distribution. My hunch, based upon the patterns of per capita income growth and poverty, is that places specialized in the information sector have had improved income distributions over the past 20 years while those specialized in the goods production and distribution sector have had worsened income distributions. What I mean by improved is that the proportion of households in the bottom classes becomes smaller over time, and by worsened I mean the opposite. That is not the same as polarization, the ratio of income for, say, the highest 10% of households to the income for the lowest 10% of households. I cannot imagine that polarization has *not* increased for all places. But the question of interest is not polarization. Rather, the question of interest is whether the proportion of households in the lower income classes has diminished (improved distribution) in some metropolitan areas and risen (worsened distribution) in other metropolitan areas, and whether those two sets of places differ in their size, specializations, and human capital. That question cannot be effectively addressed until the 2000 census data on metropolitan income distribution is available.

A second large question I have only partly addressed. Namely, is the economic viability of the central city enhanced by some metropolitanwide specializations and diminished by others? If manufacturing and distribution have become much less tied to cities while the two producer service groups continue to be concentrated in the central business districts of cities, then one would expect that places specialized in producer services would have more viable city economies. The city population data from 2000 shows that more big cities were growing than declining between 1990 and 2000 and that city growth is associated with metropolitan specialization in producer services or distribution. But population data alone is not sufficient information with which to address that issue. A thorough analysis must await publication of the social and economic data for large cities in the 2000 Census.

Policies for the Public Sector

In the nineteenth century the federal government had a central role in building the railroads that pulled the far-flung parts of the nation into a single market. That economic unification no doubt was an important factor in the income convergence among states over a century. Similarly, in the first half of the twentieth century, electric power and telephone service became ubiquitous, not because of the market but because of the pro-active stance of the federal government. The interstate highway system is as important as the railroads were in linking all of the major metropolitan areas, and it was built by the federal government. Airport construction has also been subsidized by the federal government. The railroads, the telephone, electric power, highways, and airports have all been crucial infrastructure for the development of a modern economy, particularly for the goods production and distribution sector. But now the information sector is as big as the goods production and distribution sector. It does not require the rapid, efficient transportation of goods as much as the rapid, efficient communication of information. With today's technology, that means building the fiber optic network that will link all metropolitan areas for the rapid, efficient communication of information. Private firms had been building that network, until the high-tech stock market crash in 2000–2001, without significant participation by the federal government. That is a big mistake. Boston has not been bypassed. Youngstown might be. The problem with letting the private sector build the fiber optic national network is that numerous smaller metropolitan areas might be left out of the network as the telecommunications firms rush to wire the most lucrative, that is, the biggest, metropolitan markets. Just as places bypassed by the interstate highway system have become economic backwaters, so too will the places bypassed by the fiber optic network. The expanding information sector favors large places over small, and places with high levels of human capital rather than low levels. The evidence of metropolitan income divergence over the past quarter-century reveals that the "winners" (richer places with above average long-term income growth) tend to be large places with high levels of human capital. The "losers" (poorer places with below average long-term income growth) tend to be small places with low levels of human capital. In order to level the playing field, or better yet, to provide equal opportunity for *places* in the competition for information sector establishments, the federal government, through regulation, should insure that small places have the same access at the same cost to the high-speed wide-band national fiber optic network, the railroad of the twenty-first century. That may require cross-subsidies, which is preferable to having the U.S. government foot the bill. Even if the regulatory and pricing mechanism hammered out to assure access for all metropolitan territory involves federal expenditure, it would be a sound public investment. Without such wide access to the network, we might see more decades of income divergence as small metropolitan areas become less attractive than they are now as locations for information sector establishments. There is no more important role for the federal government in promoting economic development opportunity for *all* metropolitan areas.

There are other federal policies that would foster expansion of the information sector. They include more vigorous efforts to lower international trade barriers for trade in information services, and stronger enforcement of legal protections for patents, trademarks, royalties, and license fees. Nations whose firms pirate everything from computer software to books and music CDs should be clobbered with more serious trade sanctions. That would require stiffer rules and stronger enforcement negotiated through the World Trade Organization.

A central fact that has emerged from this study is that a college-educated work force is far more important for the information sector than for the other parts of the economy. The states are the major source of public spending for higher education. In 1996, states spent $51 billion on higher education, or about 25% more than they spent in 1980. The same year, the states spent $27 billion for "correction," new-speak for incarceration, or 514% more than they spent in 1980 (U.S. Census Bureau 1999). Clearly prisons are a growth industry for state governments, but higher education is not. That is another big mistake. For all their concern with economic development, state governments have been starving their colleges to feed their prison growth. Expanding the pool of college-educated workers is important for further growth of the information sector. Expanding the pool of "corrected" workers is not. The best single policy that state governments could pursue to enhance economic growth for the information sector is improvement in the quality of and the access to higher education. That means significantly higher expenditures. Given the mobility of the college-educated population, much of the economic benefits from such improvements would spillover to other states, a fact that discourages larger state expenditures for higher education. The solution to that problem is for the federal government to become a far more significant funder than it is now of higher education. Universities are important to the information sector not just as the producers of college graduates. As Castells and Hall (1994) have noted, "as generators of new knowledge, basic and applied, research-oriented universities are to the informational economy what coal mines were to the industrial economy" (p. 231). Thus, expanded funding for higher education by state and federal governments should be not just for undergraduate education but also for research in science, engineering, and medicine.

This book has focused upon metropolitan areas as the basic unit of the subnational economy, not states or cities. But there is no one government in charge of a metropolitan area. Hence, if the above analysis points to policies that may enhance economic growth of metropolitan areas, they can only be pursued through collaborative efforts of the local governments in a metropolitan area, encouraged, or coerced, by the state government(s). How that might be achieved is someone else's department. If in fact it is the metropolitan economy that matters, not the central city's or the neighborhood's, or that of the new "edge city," then the best single policy for a city and its suburbs to pursue is to eschew all beggar-thy-neighbor economic development nostrums. Tax abatements and other public giveaways to lure firms tend to be institutionalized across jurisdictions in a state. Consequently, they cancel each other out. They do, however, transfer scarce public revenues to private firms. If the tax dollars spent by local governments in the same metropolitan area in bidding wars for firms could instead be pooled to fund area-wide economic development projects, admittedly a most unlikely scenario, that would be a first step in the right direction. Given the above analysis, what projects should be funded? Projects that encourage the expansion of and enhance the competitiveness of the information sector without killing off what remains of the goods production and distribution sector inside cities. In many old cities, expansion of producer service firms, hospitals, and universities (all parts of the information sector) plus new or restored housing for their "yuppie" employees, push up real estate values, which in turn pushes out or pushes over the edge small manufacturing and distribution establishments that had a profitable niche in the city. Relocation assistance to such firms, for relocation within the metropolitan area, would be a good use of metropolitanwide economic development dollars. It does not matter if such firms leave the old central city. What matters is that they stay in the metropolitan area.

One of the bells-and-whistles economic development projects that should be pursued is construction of all of the local telecommunication infrastructure required to gain maximum benefit from the national fiber optic network. That may mean hard-nosed negotiation with cable and telephone companies so that the entire metropolitan area can reap the future benefits, not just downtown, not just the new "edge city." Most of the things that local government, especially big-city government, can do to encourage and facilitate an expanding information sector are prosaic, affording few photo-ops. On the other hand they do not require metropolitanwide cooperation, and so are more easily attainable. Because the information sector is top-heavy with college-educated workers, cities need to please that constituency, even if many of them live in the suburbs. That means creating an environment that offers high-quality public schools, including magnet schools for outstanding students, as in New York City; a low crime rate; efficient public services; good transportation, including public transportation to an airport with more than one carrier; and the social and cultural amenities that are demanded by the college educated. Some might argue that this short list of policies for mayors to pursue is not sensitive to the needs of poor minorities in cities, but as the chief victims of bad schools, high crime, and poor transportation, the poor minorities in cities would certainly benefit from such improvements. Specifically for the poor and low-income households, I would add affordable housing programs and vigorous enforcement of building codes. The major benefit cities can provide to poor minorities, and indeed to all the urban poor, is employment. That is why city poverty rates are lower in metropolitan areas that have had stronger employment growth in the recent past. Employment growth is associated with greater specialization in the information sector, while employment decline is associated with greater specialization in the goods production and distribution sector. So, mayors who wish to improve the life chances of the urban poor would be best advised to provide a civic environment that enhances and encourages expansion of the information sector.

In light of the destruction of the World Trade Center by terrorists, with a loss of civilian lives unprecedented in this country, many firms and their employees are no doubt rethinking their attachment to big cities. Should they choose to disperse their operations to many smaller places, as manufacturing firms have done over the past decades, they would lose the tremendous agglomeration economies that apparently accrue to information sector firms clustered together in large urban places. The critical face-to-face interactions of information sector workers, so smoothly facilitated in the downtowns of big cities, would diminish. Fax machines, e-mail, teleconferencing, and telephones are not good substitutes for meetings, planned and serendipitous. If they were, we would have seen dispersion of information sector firms already. We have not. Office rents in gritty, cold Manhattan and Chicago continue to be well above office rents in Santa Barbara and other exquisitely lovely small, warm places. Why? Because the gains from location in major urban centers must far outweigh the costs for information sector firms. We cannot afford to dismantle the concentration of information sector firms in our largest cities.

| Appendix

Industry Composition of Six Traded Goods and Services Groups, by Standard Industrial Classification Code

SIC CODE

Goods Production and Distribution Sector (GP&D)

Primary Production (PRM)

Agriculture, forestry, and fisheries	01–09
Mining	10–14

Manufacturing (MFG)

Food and kindred products	20
Tobacco	21
Textiles	22
Apparel	23
Lumber and wood products	24
Furniture and fixtures	25
Paper and allied products	26
Printing and publishing	27
Chemicals and allied products	28
Petroleum and coal products	29

Rubber and miscellaneous plastic products	30
Leather and leather products	31
Stone, clay, and glass products	32
Primary metals	33
Fabricated metals	34
Industrial machinery and equipment	35
Electronic and other electrical equipment	36
Transportation equipment	37
Instruments and related products	38
Miscellaneous manufacturing	39

Distribution (DIST)

Railroad transportation	40
Trucking and warehousing	42
Water transportation	44
Transportation by air	45
Pipelines except natural gas	46
Wholesale trade	50–51

Information Sector

Financial Producer Services (PSFIN)

Depository institutions	60
Nondepository institutions	61
Security and commodity brokers	62
Insurance carriers	63
Insurance agents and brokers	64
Real estate	65
Holding and other investment offices	67

Other Producer Services (PSOTH)

Communication	48
Business services	73
Legal services	81

Population of Central Cities in Large Metropolitan Areas,
1970, 1990, and 2000 (ranked by 2000 population)

	Population (thousands)			Population Change	
	1970	1990	2000	1970–1990	1990–2000
New York	7,896	7,323	8,008	−573	686
Los Angeles	2,812	3,485	3,695	673	209
Chicago	3,369	2,784	2,896	−585	112
Houston	1,234	1,631	1,954	397	323
Philadelphia	1,949	1,586	1,518	−363	−68
Phoenix	584	983	1,321	399	338
San Diego	697	1,111	1,223	414	113
Dallas	844	1,007	1,189	163	182
San Antonio	654	936	1,145	282	209
Detroit	1,514	1,028	951	−486	−77
Indianapolis	737	731	782	−6	51
San Francisco	716	724	777	8	53
Jacksonville, FL	504	635	736	131	100
Columbus	540	633	711	93	79
Austin	254	466	657	212	191
Memphis	624	610	650	−14	40
Milwaukee	717	628	597	−89	−31
Boston	641	574	589	−67	15
Washington	757	607	572	−150	−35
Seattle	531	516	563	−15	47
Denver	515	468	555	−47	87
Nashville-Davidson	426	488	546	62	57
Charlotte	241	396	541	155	145
Portland, OR	380	437	529	57	92
Oklahoma City	368	445	506	77	61
New Orleans	593	497	485	−96	−12
Las Vegas	126	258	478	132	220
Cleveland	751	506	478	−245	−27
Atlanta	495	394	416	−101	22
Sacramento	257	369	407	112	38
Minneapolis	434	368	383	−66	14
Miami	335	359	362	24	4
St. Louis	622	397	348	−225	−48
Pittsburgh	520	370	335	−150	−35
Cincinnati	454	364	331	−90	−33
Tampa	278	280	303	2	23
Buffalo	463	328	293	−135	−35
Raleigh	123	208	276	85	68
Norfolk	308	261	234	−47	−27
Greensboro	144	184	224	40	40
Rochester, NY	295	232	220	−63	−12
Grand Rapids	198	189	198	−9	9
Orlando	99	165	186	66	21
Salt Lake City	176	160	182	−16	22
Kansas City, MO	507	150	147	−357	−3
Hartford	158	140	122	−18	−18
TOTAL	36,840	36,409	39,618	−431	3,209

Source: U.S. Census Bureau 1989, 2000.

| References

Abu-Lughod, Janet L. 1999. *New York, Chicago, Los Angeles: America's Global Cities.* Minneapolis: University of Minnesota Press.

Advertising Age. 2000. April 24.

Aley, Howard C. 1949. *Our Neighbors Tell Us about Their Work,* Chicago: R. P. Donnelley and Sons.

Arrow, Kenneth J. 1962. "The Economic Implications of Learning by Doing." *Review of Economic Studies* 29:155–173.

Baily, Martin Neil, and Robert Z. Lawrence. 2001. "Do We Have a New E-conomy?" *American Economic Review* 91–92:308–312.

Bairoch, Paul 1988. *Cities and Economic Development.* Chicago: University of Chicago Press.

Barro, Robert J., and Xavier Sala-I-Martin. 1991. "Convergence across States and Regions." *Brookings Papers on Economic Activity* 1:107–182.

Baumol, William J. 1967. "Macroeconomics of Unbalanced Growth: The Anatomy of Urban Crisis." *American Economic Review* 57:415–426.

Baumol, William J., L. Osberg, and N. Wolff. 1989. *The Information Economy: The Implications of Unbalanced Growth.* Halifax: Institute for Research on Public Policy.

BEA (Bureau of Economic Analysis). 1979 (April). *Survey of Current Business.* Vol. 59, no. 4, "Input-Output Accounts for the U.S. Economy, 1972," Table 1.

———. 1997a (November). *Survey of Current Business.* Vol. 77, no. 11, "Benchmark Input-Output Accounts for the U.S. Economy, 1992," 36–82.

———. 1997b (November). *Survey of Current Business,* Vol. 77, no. 11, "Gross Product by Industry, 1947–96," 20–34.

———. 1998a (May). Regional Economic Information System (REIS) CD-ROM, Washington, DC: Economics and Statistics Administration, U.S. Department of Commerce.

———. 1998b (October). National Income and Product Accounts, disk BE-54.

——. 1999a (July). *Survey of Current Business*. Vol. 79, no. 7, p. 12.

——. 1999b (October). *Survey of Current Business*. Vol. 79, no. 10, "U.S. International Services," 48–89.

——. 1999c (December). *Survey of Current Business*. Vol. 79, no. 12, "National Income and Product Accounts," Table 6.1C, p. 87.

——. 2000a (January). *Survey of Current Business*. Vol. 80, no. 1, "Input-Output Accounts for the U.S. Economy, 1996," Table 2, pp. 56–65.

——. 2000b (January). "U.S. International Transactions," Tables 1 and 2, Web site www.bea.doc.gov.

——. 2000c (June). *Survey of Current Business*. Vol. 80, no. 6.

——. 2000d (July). *Survey of Current Business*. Vol. 80, no. 7, "U.S. Multinational Companies' Operations in 1998." Table 5, p. 32, and Table 10.2, p. 38.

——. 2001a (May). Regional Economic Information System (REIS) CD-ROM, Washington, DC: Economics and Statistics Administration, U.S. Department of Commerce.

——. 2001b (July). *Survey of Current Business*. Vol. 81, no. 7, "U.S. International Transactions, First Quarter 2001," Tables 1, 2, 3, pp. 46–65.

——. 2001c (September). *Survey of Current Business*. Vol. 81, no. 9, "Foreign Direct Investment in the United States," Table 17, pp. 76–77.

Beauregard, Robert A., and Anne Haila. 2000. "The Unavoidable Continuities of the City." In *Globalizing Cities: A New Spatial Order?*, ed. Peter Marcuse and Ronald van Kempen. Oxford: Blackwell.

Beckmann, Martin J. 1981. "Land Use Then and Now: A Tribute to Sir James Steuart," *Papers, Regional Science Association* 48:1–6.

Bell, Daniel. 1973. *The Coming of Post-Industrial Society: A Venture in Social Forecasting*. New York: Basic Books.

Beyers, William. 1992. "Producer Services and Metropolitan Growth and Development." In *Sources of Metropolitan Growth*, ed. Edwin Mills and John McDonald. New Brunswick, NJ: Rutgers University Press.

Black, Duncan, and J. Vernon Henderson. 1999. "Spatial Evolution of Population and Industry in the U.S." *American Economic Review* 89:2, 321–327.

Black, John. 1997. *A Dictionary of Economics*. Oxford: Oxford University Press.

Blanchard, Olivier Jean, and Lawrence F. Katz. 1992. "Regional Evolutions." *Brookings Papers on Economic Activity* 1:1–75.

Blue, F. J., William D. Jenkins, H. William Larsen, and J. M. Reedy. 1995. *Mahoning Memories*. Virginia Beach, VA: Donning.

Bluestone, Barry, and Mary Huff Stevenson. 2000. *The Boston Renaissance*. New York: Russell Sage Foundation.

Borts, George H. 1960. "The Equalization of Returns and Regional Economic Growth." *American Economic Review* 50:319–347.

Borts, George H., and J. L. Stein 1964. *Economic Growth in a Free Market*. New York: Columbia University Press.

Bureau of Economic Analysis. *See* BEA.

Capello, R. 1994. "Towards New Industrial and Spatial Systems: The Role of New Technologies," *Papers in Regional Science* 73:189–208.

Carlino, Gerald A. 1992. "Are Regional Per Capita Earnings Diverging?" *Business Review,* Federal Reserve Bank of Philadelphia, March–April, 3–12.

Castells, Manuel. 1989. *The Informational City.* Oxford: Basil Blackwell.

———. 1996. *The Rise of the Network Society.* Vol. 1 of *The Information Age.* Oxford: Blackwell.

Castells, Manuel, and Peter Hall. 1994. *Technopoles of the World.* London: Routledge.

Cheshire, Paul, and Edwin S. Mills, eds. 1999. "Applied Urban Economics." *Handbook of Regional and Urban Economics, Volume 3.* Amsterdam: Elsevier Science, North Holland.

Chinitz, Benjamin. 1961. "Contrasts in Agglomeration: New York and Pittsburgh." *American Economic Review* 57:415–426.

Clark, Colin. 1951. *The Conditions of Economic Progress.* London: Macmillan.

Coffey, William J., and Mario Polese. 1989. "Producer Services and Regional Development: A Policy-Oriented Perspective." *Papers of the Regional Science Association* 67:13–27.

Conservation of Human Resources. 1977. *The Corporate Headquarters Complex in New York City.* Montclair, NJ: Allanheld Osmun.

Daniels, Peter W. 1985. *Service Industries: A Geographical Appraisal.* London: Methuen.

Downs, Anthony. 1997. "The Challenge of Our Declining Big Cities." *Housing Policy Debate* 8, no. 2: 359–408.

Drennan, Matthew P. 1989. "Information Intensive Industries in Metropolitan Areas of the United States. *Environment and Planning A* 21:1603–1618.

———. 1992. "Gateway Cities: The Metropolitan Sources of U.S. Producer Service Exports." *Urban Studies* 29:217–235.

———. 1996. "The Changing Economic Functions of the New York Region." In *Research in Urban Economics.* Vol. 10, *New Urban Strategies in Advanced Regional Economies,* ed. R. D. Norton. Greenwich, CT: JAI Press.

———. 1999. "National Structural Change and Metropolitan Specialization in the United States." *Papers in Regional Science* 78:297–318.

———. 2000a. "New York: Demography, Labour Force and Income." In *London–New York Study.* London: The Corporation of London.

———. 2000b. "New York: Business and Professional Services." In *London–New York Study.* London: The Corporation of London.

Drennan, Matthew P., Shannon Larsen, José Lobo, Deborah Strumsky, and Wahyu Utomo. Forthcoming. "Sectoral Shares, Specialization, and Metropolitan Wages in the United States, 1969–1996." *Urban Studies.*

Drennan, Matthew P., and José Lobo. 1997. "U.S. Metropolitan Economic Growth, 1969–1989: The Roles of Human Capital, Trade, and Specialization." Working Paper, Department of City and Regional Planning, Cornell University.

———. 1999. "A Simple Test for Convergence of Metropolitan Income in the United States." *Journal of Urban Economics* 46:350–359.

———. Forthcoming. "An Application of the Unit Root Test to the Question of Income Convergence across U.S. Metropolitan Areas."

Drennan, Matthew P., Emmanuel Tobier, and Jonathan Lewis. 1996. "The Interruption of Income Convergence and Income Growth in Large Cities in the 1980s." *Urban Studies* 33:63–82.

Dun and Bradstreet. 1999. *Consulting Directory.*

Dunford, Martin, Jack Holland, and Phil Lee. 1994. *Holland, Belgium, and Luxembourg: The Rough Guide.* London: Rough Guides.

Ehrenberg, Ronald G., and Robert S. Smith. 2000. *Modern Labor Economics: Theory and Public Policy,* 6th ed. Reading, MA: Addison Wesley.

Esparza, A., and A. Krmenec. 1996. "The Spatial Extent of Producer Service Markets: Hierarchical Models of Interaction Revisited." *Papers in Regional Science* 75: 375–395.

Fainstein, Susan S., and Michael Harloe. 1992. "Introduction: London and New York in the Contemporary World." In *Divided Cities,* ed. Susan S. Fainstein, Ian Gordon, and Michael Harloe. Cambridge, MA: Blackwell.

Fisher, A. G. B. 1935. *The Clash of Progress and Security.* London: Macmillan.

Fortune. 1995. "The *Fortune* 1,000." April.

———. 2001. "The *Fortune* 1,000." April.

Friedman, Milton. 1992. "Do Old Fallacies Ever Die?" *Journal of Economic Literature* 30:2129–2132.

Garcia-Mila, Teresa, and Therese J. McGuire. 1998. "A Note on the Shift to a Service-Based Economy and the Consequences for Regional Growth." *Journal of Regional Science* 38:353–363.

Garnick, D. H. 1990. "Accounting for Regional Differences in Per Capita Personal Income Growth." *Survey of Current Business* 70:29–40.

Gaspar, Jess, and Edward L. Glaeser. 1998. "Information Technology and the Future of Cities." *Journal of Urban Economics* 43:136–156.

Geirnaert, Noel, and Ludo Vandamme. 1996. *Bruges: Two Thousand Years of History.* Bruges: Stichting Kunstboek.

Glaeser, Edward. 1994. "Cities, Information and Economic Growth." *Cityscape* 1:9–47.

Glaeser, Edward, H. D. Kallal, J. A. Scheinkman, and A. Shleifer. 1992. "Growth in Cities." *Journal of Political Economy* 100:1126–1152.

Glaeser, Edward, J. A. Scheinkman, and A. Shleifer. 1995. "Economic Growth in a Cross-Section of Cities." *Journal of Monetary Economics* 36:117–143.

Gottmann, Jean. 1961. *Megalopolis: The Urbanized Northeastern Seaboard of the United States.* Twentieth Century Fund. Cambridge, MA: MIT Press.

Greenfield, H. I. 1966. *Manpower and the Growth of Producer Services.* New York: Columbia University Press.

Haig, R. M. 1926. "Toward an Understanding of the Metropolis: I. Some Speculations regarding the Economic Basis of Urban Concentrations." *Quarterly Journal of Economics* 40:179–208.

Hansen, Niles. 1990. "Do Producer Services Induce Regional Economic Development?" *Journal of Regional Science* 30:465–476.

Henderson, J. Vernon. 1988. *Urban Development: Theory, Fact and Illusion.* Oxford: Oxford University Press.

Henderson, J. Vernon, A. Kuncoro, and M. Turner. 1995. "Industrial Development in Cities." *Journal of Political Economy* 103:1067–1090.

Institutional Investor. 1999. August.

Jacobs, Jane. 1961. *The Death and Life of Great American Cities.* New York: Random House.

———. 1969. *The Economy of Cities.* New York: Vintage Books.

Jargowsky, Paul. 1997. *Poverty and Place.* New York: Russell Sage.

Jones, Barclay. 1984. "Productivity and the Spatial Implications of Structural Change: Empirical Evidence for Simon's Model." *Papers of the Regional Science Association* 54:1–11.

Kenney, Nathaniel T. 1959. "New Era on the Great Lakes." *National Geographic* 115:439–490.

Knobe, William. 1996. *Bold New World: The Essential Road Map to the Twenty-First Century.* New York: Kodansha.

Krugman, Paul. 2001. "Chip of Fools." *New York Times,* April 18, A23.

Ladd, Helen, and John Yinger. 1989. *America's Ailing Cities.* Baltimore: Johns Hopkins University Press.

Landes, David S. 1998. *The Wealth and Poverty of Nations.* New York: W. W. Norton.

Levy, Frank. 1998. *The New Dollars and Dreams.* New York: Russell Sage Foundation.

Logan, John, Peter Taylor-Gooby, and Monika Reuter. 1992. "Poverty and Income Inequality." In *Divided Cities,* ed. Susan S. Fainstein, Ian Gordon, and Michael Harloe. Cambridge, MA: Blackwell.

Lucas, Robert E., Jr., 1990. "Why Doesn't Capital Flow from Rich to Poor Countries?" *American Economic Review Papers and Proceedings* 80:92–96.

Machlup, Fritz. 1962. *The Production and Distribution of Knowledge in the United States.* Princeton: Princeton University Press.

Madden, Janice F. 2000. *Changes in Income Inequality within U.S. Metropolitan Areas.* Kalamazoo, MI: W. E. Upjohn Institute for Employment Research.

Maharidge, Dale. 1985. *Journey to Nowhere.* New York: Hyperion.

Marcuse, Peter, and Ronald van Kempen, eds. 2000. "Introduction." In *Globalizing Cities: A New Spatial Order?* Oxford: Blackwell.

Marshall, Alfred. 1890. *Principles of Economics.* London: Macmillan.

Marshall, J. N. 1986. *Uneven Development in the Service Economy: Understanding the Location and Role of Producer Services.* Institute of British Geographers.

Mills, Edwin S. 1988. "Service Sector Suburbanization." In *America's New Market Geography,* ed. George Sternlieb and James W. Hughes. New Brunswick, NJ: Center for Urban Policy Research.

Mollenkopf, John H., and Manuel Castells, eds. 1991. "Introduction." In *Dual City.* New York: Russell Sage Foundation.

Naisbitt, John. 1994. *The Global Paradox*. New York: Avon Books.

Negroponte, Nicholas. 1995. *Being Digital*. New York: Vintage Books.

New York State Department of Labor. 2000 (December). *Employment Review* 53:94–95.

New York Times. 2000. "As Dot-Coms Retrench, Financial Firms Fill Their Space," November 5, p. 55.

Nicholas, David. 1997. *The Later Medieval City*. London: Longmans.

Norton, R. D. 1986. "Industrial Policy and American Renewal." *Journal of Economic Literature* 24:1–40.

Noyelle, Thierry J., and Penny Peace. 1991. "Information Industries: New York's New Export Base." In *Services and Metropolitan Development*, ed. Peter Daniels. London: Routledge.

Noyelle, Thierry J., and Thomas M. Stanback, Jr. 1984. *The Economic Transformation of American Cities*. Totowa, NJ: Rowman and Allanheld.

Office of Technology Assessment, U.S. Congress. 1995. "The Technological Reshaping of Metropolitan America." OTA-ETI 643, September.

Perloff, Harvey S. 1963. *How a Region Grows*. New York: Committee for Economic Development.

Porat, M. 1977. *The Information Economy: Definition and Measurement*. Special Publication 77-12(1). Office of Telecommunications. Washington, DC: U.S. Department of Commerce.

Porter, Michael E. 1990. *The Competitive Advantage of Nations*. New York: Free Press.

Pred, Allan. 1977. *City Systems in Advanced Economies*. New York: Halsted Press.

Quigley, John M. 1998. "Urban Diversity and Economic Growth." *Journal of Economic Perspectives* 12:127–138.

Rauch, James E. 1993. "Productivity Gains from Geographic Concentration of Human Capital: Evidence from the Cities." *Journal of Urban Economics* 34:380–400.

Roemer, Paul M. 1986. "Increasing Returns and Long-Run Growth." *Journal of Political Economy* 94:1002–1037.

Rosenberg, Nathan. 1963. "Technological Change in the Machine Tool Industry, 1840–1910." *Journal of Economic History* 23:414–443.

Rowthorn, Robert, and Ramana Ramaswamy. 1997. "Deindustrialization: Causes and Implications." International Monetary Fund Working Paper, April.

Rusk, David. 1995. *Cities Without Suburbs*, 2nd ed. Washington, DC: Woodrow Wilson Center Press.

Sale, Kirkpatrick. 1975. *Power Shift: The Rise of the Southern Rim and Its Challenge to the Eastern Establishment*. New York: Random House.

Sassen, Saskia 1991. *The Global City: New York, London, Tokyo*. Princeton: Princeton University Press.

———. 2001. *The Global City: New York, London, Tokyo,* 2nd ed. Princeton: Princeton University Press.

Scherer, Frederic M. 1982. "Inter-Industry Technology Flows in the United States." *Resource Policy* 11:227–245.

Schumpeter, Joseph A. 1942. *Capitalism, Socialism, and Democracy*. New York: Harper.

Schwartz, Alex. 1993. "Subservant Suburbia: Reliance of Large Suburban Companies on Central City Firms." *Journal of the American Planning Association* 59:3, 288–305.

Scott, Allen J. 1998. *Regions and the World Economy*. Oxford: Oxford University Press.

Scott, Allen J., and Michael Storper. 1986. "Industrial Change and Territorial Organization: A Summing Up." In *Production, Work, Territory*, ed. A. Scott and M. Storper. Boston: Allen and Unwin.

Simon, Curtis J. 1998. "Human Capital and Metropolitan Employment Growth." *Journal of Urban Economics* 43:223–243.

Simon, Herbert A. 1947. "Effects of Increased Productivity upon the Ratio of Urban to Rural Population." *Econometrica* 12:599–606.

———. 1982. "The Rural-Urban Population Balance Again." *Regional Science and Urban Economics* 12:599–606.

Singlemann, J. 1974. "The Sectoral Transformation of the Labor Force in Seven Industrialized Countries, 1920–1960." Ph.D. diss., University of Texas.

Singlemann, J., and H. L. Browning. 1980. "Industrial Transformation and Occupational Change in the U.S., 1960–1970." *Social Forces* 59:246–264.

Stanback, Thomas M., Jr., Peter J. Bearse, Thierry J. Noyelle, and Robert Karasek. 1981. *Services: The New Economy*. Totowa, NJ: Allanheld Osmun.

Stigler, George. 1961. "The Economics of Information." *The Journal of Political Economy* 69:213–225.

Storper, Michael. 1997. *The Regional World*. New York: Guilford Press.

"Supplementary Tables." 2002. Available on line at www.crp.cornell.edu/publications/facultypubs/drennan/Supplementlist.html and www.press.jhu.edu/press/books/titles/s02/s02drin.htm.

Toffler, Alvin. 1980. *The Third Wave*, New York: Morrow.

U.S. Census Bureau. 1989. *Statistical Abstract of the United States: 1989*, 109th ed. Washington, DC.

———. 1998. *County Business Patterns 1996 New York*.

———. 1999. *Statistical Abstract of the United States: 1999*. 119th ed. Washington, DC.

———. 2000. Internet site www.census.gov/population/estimates/state.

U.S. Department of Housing and Urban Development. 1999. *Now Is the Time: Places Left Behind in the New Economy*. Washington, DC.

U.S. Department of Labor, Bureau of Labor Statistics. 1999. *Occupational Employment Statistics*. Computer disk.

Ward's Business Directory. 1999.

Wilson, William Julius. 1987. *The Truly Disadvantaged: The Inner City, the Underclass, and Public Policy*. Chicago: University of Chicago Press.

———. 1996. *When Work Disappears*. New York: Vintage Books.

Wood, Peter A. 1987. "Producer Services and Economic Change: U.K. Reflections on Canadian Evidence." In *Technological Change and Industrial Policy*, ed. K. Chapman and G. Humphrey. London: Blackwell.

Yeoman, Barry. 2000. "Steel Town Lockdown." *Mother Jones*, May–June, 38–47.

| Index

dividends, income from, 69, 74
dot-com stocks, 50–51, 53–54
Downs, Anthony, 129
Drennan, Matthew P., 17, 24, 57, 60, 73, 82, 83, 90, 113, 120

earnings
concentrations of metropolitan, 61–64
data, 59–61
distribution of, in metropolitan areas, 55–56
specialization of metropolitan, 67–71
of traded goods and services groups, 32–33
Ehernberg, Ronald, 5
employment
data, 59–61
in *Fortune* 1,000 firms, 42–43
growth in, 101–103, 107–109, 110
by occupation, 24–27
in traded goods and services groups, 32–34
Esparza, A., 17
evolution of economies, 19–20

Fainstein, Susan S., 121
federal monies to states, 31
fiber optic network, 132–133, 135
financial producer services
definition of, 16–19
industries included in, 138
Fisher, A. G. B., 20
foreign direct investment, 48–49
foreign trade, 44–47
Fortune 1,000, 42–44
Friedman, Milton, 114

Garcia-Mila, Teresa, 40
Garnick, D. H., 73, 113
Gaspar, Jess, 8, 71–72
Geirnaert, Noel, 1, 2
Glaeser, Edward, 8, 57, 60, 71–72, 73, 84, 86, 87, 113
goods production and distribution sector
and central city growth, 80–82
and employment growth, 101–103
evolution of, 9

foreign direct investment in, 48–49
growth of, 32–35
and income divergence, 116–119
and income growth, 97–99
and income level, 93–97, 109
in input-output accounts, 36–42
and international trade, 44–46
large firms in, 42–44
measurement of, 32
in metropolitan areas, 55–56
multinational corporations in, 47–48
occupations in, 25–26
and population growth, 99–101
size of, 7, 32–35
and stock market decline, 51–54
and traded goods, 6
and urban poverty, 122–129
Gordon, Ian, 121
Gottmann, Jean, 16, 20–21, 22
Greenfield, H. I., 23
Greenspan, Alan, 53

Haig, M., 20
Haila, Anne, 122
Hall, Peter, 3
Hansen, Niles, 17, 24
Harloe, Michael, 121
health industry, 30–31
Henderson, J. Vernon, 22, 57, 60, 61, 62, 78, 86
high-tech stocks, 49–54
human capital
and city poverty, 126–129
correlation of, with other variables, 95–97
and employment growth, 103, 107–109, 111
and income divergence, 10–11, 117–118
and income growth, 97–99, 105, 110
and income level, 93, 110
and metropolitan specialization, 68, 73–74
and public policies, 134

income, per capita
and correlation, 95–97
growth, 90, 97–99, 105–106